W9-APY-721

WORLD OF MAN

A LIBRARY OF THEORY AND RESEARCH IN THE HUMAN SCIENCES

Editor: R. D. Laing

The Politics of the Family
and Other Essays

The Politics
of the Family
and Other Essays

R. D. LAING

VINTAGE BOOKS

A Division of Random House
New York

VINTAGE BOOKS EDITION, September 1972

Copyright © 1969, 1971 by The R. D. Laing Trust
Originally published in the United States by Pantheon Books, a
division of Random House, Inc., in 1969.
Part of the material in this book was originally published in 1969 in
Canada by Canadian Broadcasting Corporation. This revised edition
is also published by Canadian Broadcasting Corporation in Canada
and by Tavistock Publications, London.

Library of Congress Cataloging in Publication Data
Laing, Ronald David.
The Politics of the Family.
Original ed. issued in series: World of man.
Includes bibliographical references.
1. Family—Addresses, essays, lectures. I. Title.
HQ728.L335 1972   301.42′08   72–1118
ISBN 0–394–71809–7

Manufactured in the United States of America

Contents

Preface

This book consists of revisions of talks (except the first chapter) given in 1967–68 on diverse occasions. I have eliminated many redundancies, leaving, I hope, not too many, and tidied up the English. The first chapter is virtually rewritten. Otherwise they are as they were: intended, then and now, to evoke questions rather than to provide answers.

From 1961 to 1967 my studies of families were supported by Fellowships from the Foundations Fund for Research in Psychiatry (Grant No 64–297) and the Tavistock Institute of Human Relations.

London, March 1971   R. D. Laing

LAWS I

ATHENIAN: ... assuming that you have reasonably good laws, one of the best of them will be the law forbidding any young men to enquire which of them are right or wrong; but with one mouth and one voice they must all agree that the laws are all good, for they come from God; and any one who says the contrary is not to be listened to. But an old man who remarks any defect in your laws may communicate his observation to a ruler or to an equal in years when no young man is present.

CLEINAS: Exactly so, Stranger; and like a diviner, although not there at the time, you seem to me quite to have hit the meaning of the legislator ...

ATHENIAN: ... we may observe that any speculation about laws turns almost entirely on pleasure and pain, both in states and in individuals ...

LAWS IV

ATHENIAN: ... we must ... regulate our cities and houses according to law, meaning by the very term 'law', the distribution of mind.

Plato, *Laws* (Jowett translation)

Part I
Essays

The Family and the 'Family'[1]

We speak of families as though we all knew what families
are. We identify, as families, networks of people who live
together over periods of time, who have ties of marriage and kinship to one another. The more one studies
family dynamics, the more *un*clear one becomes as to
the ways *family* dynamics compare and contrast with the
dynamics of other groups not called families, let alone the
ways families themselves differ. As with dynamics, so
with structure (patterns, more stable and enduring than
others): again, comparisons and generalizations must be
very tentative.

The dynamics and structures found in those groups called
families in our society may not be evident in those groups
called families in other places and times. The relevance of the
dynamics and structure of the family to the formation of
personality is unlikely to be constant in different societies,
or even in our own.

The family here discussed is the family of origin transformed by internalization, partitioning, and other operations, into the 'family'[2] and mapped back onto the family
and elsewhere. It is to the relation between the observable

---

[1] Revised from 'Individual and Family Structure' in Lomas (1967).

[2] Single inverted commas are used when it is necessary to make clear
that it is the internalized family that is in question.

3

structures of the family and the structures that endure as part of the 'family' as a set of relations and operations between them that this chapter is addressed.

THE FAMILY AS FANTASY

The *family as a system* is internalized. Relations and operations between elements and sets of elements are internalized, not elements in isolation. Elements may be persons, things, or part-objects. Parents are internalized as close or apart, together or separate, near or distant, loving, fighting, etc., each other and self. Mother and father may be merged as a sort of fused parental matrix, or be broken down into segments that transect the usual personal partitions. Their sexual relation as envisaged by the child holds a sort of nuclear position in every internal 'family'. Members of the family may feel more or less in or out of any part or whole of the family, according as they feel themselves to have the family inside themselves and to be inside the set of relations characterizing the internal family of other members of the family.

The family as internalized is a space–time system. What is internalized as 'near' or 'far', 'together' or 'divorced', are not only spatial relations. A *temporal* sequence is *always* present.

If I think of others as together with me, and yet others as not together with me, I have undertaken two acts of synthesis, resulting in *we* and *them*. The family is a common *we*, in contrast to *them* outside the family. But, in addition, there are the subgroups within the family, we, me, you, them, *we* parents, *those* children, *we* children, mother-and-child *we*, and father as *him*, and so on. When I identify myself as one of us, I expect you to do likewise. When there are three, you and he or she and me, each becomes one of *us*. In such a family *we*, each of *us*, recognize(s) not only his or her own family synthesis, but expects a comparable family synthesis to exist in you, him, or her also. My 'family' comprises his or hers, is his and mine, hers and mine. The 'family' is no simple social object, shared by its members. The 'family' to each of its members is no objective set of relations. It exists in each of the elements in it, *and nowhere else*.

As Sartre would say, the family is united by the reciprocal internalization by each (whose token of membership is precisely this interiorized[1] family) of each other's internalization. The unity of the family is in the interior of each synthesis and each synthesis is bound by reciprocal interiority with each other's internalization of each other's interiorization . . .

Unification by co-inherence occurs in the Christian experience of being one 'in' Christ. Co-inherence pervaded the Nazi mystique of the Country and the Party. We feel ourselves to be One in so far as each of us has inside himself a presence common to all brothers and sisters in Christ, in the Party, or in the family.[2]

What function has 'the family' in terms of the relationship of members of the family?

The 'family', the family as a fantasy structure, entails a type of relationship between family members of a different order from the relationships of those who do not share that 'family' inside each other.

[1] Interiorize and interiorization are used synonymously with internalize and internalization.

[2] I mean to make only the most abstract of comparisons between groups based on such co-inherence. For a discussion of co-inherence from a Christian point of view, see Williams (1950).

The 'family' is not an introjected object, but an introjected set of relations.

The 'family', as an internal system one is inside, may not be clearly differentiated from other such systems, to which one can give only such very inadequate names as 'womb', 'breast', 'mother's body', and so forth. It may be felt to be alive, dying or dead, an animal, a machine, often a human protective or destructive container like the face–house–bodies children draw. This is a set of elements with partitions the self is in, *together* with others who have it in them.

The family may be imagined as a web, a flower, a tomb, a prison, a castle. Self may be more aware of an image of the family than of the family itself, and map the images onto the family.

'Family' space and time is akin to mythic space and time, in that it tends to be ordered round a centre and runs on repeating cycles. Who, what, where, is the centre of the family?

According to one description:

'My family was like a flower. Mother was the centre and we were the petals. When I broke away, mother felt that she had lost an arm. They (sibs) still meet round her like that. Father never really comes into the family in that sense.'

This family is represented by an image of an object, the function of which is to convey the experience of being part of a *vegetative* structure.

INTERNALIZATION

'Internalization' means to map 'outer' onto 'inner'. It entails the transference of a group of relations constituting a set (with a number of operations within the set between elements of the set, products remaining in the set) from one modality of experience to others: namely from perception to imagination, memory, dreams.

We perceive something in our waking life; we remember it; then we forget it; we dream of something with different content but similar structure; we remember the dream but not the original perception. From this and other kinds of internalization, some patterns recur in our reveries, dreams, imagination, fantasy. Counter-patterns may be set up in imagination against those in fantasy. Scenarios of dramatic sequences of space–time relations between elements undergo transformation (e.g. towards wish-fulfilling or catastrophic outcomes) as they recur in the different modalities. We may try to act upon our wish- or fear-fulfilling imagination of which we become aware only by suffering the effects of such action.

Dostoevsky depicts Raskolnikov's family in the interplay of his memories, dreams, unconscious fantasy, imagination, and in his actions in relation to actual others. While trying to be what he imagines, he enacts instead his fantasy pattern of his 'family', traceable through his dreams, memories, reveries, and physical experiences from which the 'he' that is doing things in this world is largely dissociated.[1]

Thus many processes are subsumed under the one word 'internalization.' These all entail transition or modulation from one mode to another.

[1] See Laing (1969).

To summarize: what is internalized are not objects as such but patterns of relationship by internal operations upon which a person develops an incarnate group structure.

TRANSFORMATION AND EXTERNALIZATION (PROJECTION)

This internal group may condition, more or less, a person's relationship to himself. Triadic relationships are collapsed into self–self relations. An adult feels like a child trying to reconcile two 'sides' of himself, pulling him in opposite directions, experienced perhaps as good or bad, as male or female, even physically, on right and left sides of the body: he tries to put ideas together, but an internal third party intervenes, and so on.

These internal self–self relations are as varied as actual family systems. Even when the 'family' does not become a major means of relating or not relating to one's 'self', one is oneself changed to some extent through having such a group inside. Some seem so to depend on such group operations to structure their space and time that, without them, they feel they would not be able to keep themselves together.

A young man feels his life has come to a stop. He is preoccupied by the conflict between East and West, the cold war, the balance of terror, techniques of deterrence, one world, the impossibility of divorce, the need for coexistence, the apparent impossibility of coexistence. He has a mission to find a solution, but he feels hopeless, and paralysed. He does nothing, but feels crushed by his responsibility for the destruction he feels is inevitable.

The structural elements of his preoccupations – conflict,

the cold war, emotional divorce, balance of terror, need for coexistence – resemble those in the relationship between his parents.

But he does not see these resemblances. He insists that his preoccupation with the world situation is not only entirely justified by objective facts but entirely based on them. The world situation is a fact and thousands of people come from families like his, *therefore* there is no connection.

A married woman dreams her husband makes flagrant love to a younger woman in front of her while she is terrified to show any jealousy. If she shows she is jealous she may be punished. She links this to her concern about a current affair of her husband. But she does not see any connections between an early weaning situation, seeing mother–father making love, mother (to whom she likens husband) and younger sister together, and a taboo in the family against any 'bad' feelings or jealous action to break up excluding twosomes.

It is impossible to assess the extent of these internal operations and transformations by psychoanalytic technique alone. Studies of families in conjunction with studies of 'families' are required.

In very disturbed people, one finds what may be regarded as delusional structures, still recognizably related to family situations. The re-projection of the 'family' is not simply a matter of projecting an 'internal' object onto an external person. It is superimposition of one set of relations onto another: the two sets may match more or less. Only if they mis-match sufficiently in the eyes of others, is the operation regarded as psychotic. That is, the operation is not regarded as psychotic *per se*.

It is never enough to think of spatial structure alone, much less of one inner object out of context. One should always look for a sequence of events in which more elements than one have their parts to play.

A man felt destroyed by a woman. He felt, when thirty, that she behaved just as his mother had done when he was three. This was not the first, nor was it to be the last, time he felt that way.

The prototype was brought to light through an analysis of its transference onto the present, then checked against collateral evidence from parents and others.

Prototypical sequence
1. He is with the woman he loves (his nanny).
2. His mother returns, sends nanny away,
3. and then sends him away to boarding school,
4. while father does not intervene.
5. Mother vacillates between him and affairs with men.
6. He runs away from boarding school and is returned by the police.

Repeating scenario as an adult
1. He falls in love with A.
2. He leaves A for B,
3. and breaks up with B.
4. C does not intervene.
5. He and B vacillate between each other and affairs with others.
6. He tries to escape but can't.

The main difference between the two sequences is that in the latter *he tries to do what was done to him*. He leaves A. B does not take him away. He drives B away. In making B leave him, he seems to be in control. But he experiences each repeat of the scenario as though he is the victim of B, and finally of the scenario, for which mother is held responsible. B took him away from A, then deserted him, then forced him into the wilderness. I looked on like his father.

The drama, 'internalized' and re-enacted with a semblance of control, is experienced as his destruction at the hands of a woman.

This 'destroyer' is an assigned role in one drama. However, there are several family dramas. When we go back in time in his life, we come across others, and when we go forward only a little the drama changes again. These different dramas are performed simultaneously in the one theatre, farce and tragedy on the same stage at once.

The scenario transformed, through reversals, mergers, partitioning, inversions, and so on, may be still recognizable. Usually, also, it is endowed with an *ending* – happy or catastrophic.

When such an internal template of space–time relations-in-sequence is externalized, it appears to function both as a schema governing ways external events are hoped, feared, seen to happen, and, by inducing action and reaction, as self-fulfilling fantasy and prophecy.

THE TRANSFERENCE OF GROUP MODES

The child is born into a family which is the product of the operations of human beings already in this world. It is a system mediated through sight, sound, taste, smell, touch, pain and pleasure, heat and cold, an ocean in which the child quickly learns to swim. But of this series, *relations*, *not simply objects*, are internalized and construed for significance.

The family described here is a group mode characterized by co-inherence. Some families are run more on organization–business lines; some are institutions. From morning to night the one person metamorphoses as he passes from one group mode to another; from family to bus queue, to business, to friends at lunch, to Old Boys' Reunion, before retiring to family. Transference entails carrying over one metamorphosis, based on being 'in' and having inside oneself one group mode of sociality, into another.

The 'family' is transferred to business. Or the tired businessman, 'business' now a product of business mapped by 'family', maps 'business' onto family.

The person who moves through different pluralities in a pluralistic society functions in different modes, even simultaneously, while each internal set of modal structures undergoes transformation different in type, phasing, tempo, etc.

THE DEFENSIVE FUNCTION OF THE 'FAMILY'

'There seems to be no agent more effective than another person in bringing a world for oneself alive, or, by a glance, a gesture, or a remark, shrivelling up the reality in which one is lodged' (Goffman, 1961).

Most defences described in psychoanalysis are intrapsychic defences – for instance: splitting, projection, introjection, denial, repression, regression. These defence mechanisms of psychoanalysis are *what a person does to himself*. They are not actions on the external world, on others, or on the world of others.

Persons do manifestly try to act on the 'inner' worlds of others to preserve their own inner worlds, and others (so-called obsessionals, for instance), arrange and rearrange the *external* world of objects to preserve their inner worlds.

There is no systematic psychoanalytic theory of the nature of *transpersonal* defences, whereby self attempts *to regulate the inner life of the other in order to preserve his own*, nor of techniques of coping with such persecution by others.

If self depends on the integrity of the 'family', the 'family' being a shared structure, self's integrity is then dependent upon self's sense of this as a structure shared with others. One feels secure if one imagines the integrity of the 'family' structure 'in' others.

Each family member incarnates a structure derived from relations between members. This family-in-common shared *group presence* exists *in so far as* each member has it inside himself. Hence fantasies of the family as preserved, destroyed, or repaired, the family growing, dying, being immortal. Each member of the family may require the other members to keep the same 'family' imago inside themselves. Each person's identity then rests on a shared 'family' inside the others, who, by that token, are themselves in the same family. *To be in the same family is to feel the same 'family' inside*.

In some families parents cannot allow children to break the 'family' down within themselves, if that is what they want to do, because this is felt as the breakup of the family, and then where will it end? For the child also the 'family' may be an internal structure more important then the 'breast', 'penis', 'mother' or 'father'. As long as the 'family' is felt as permanent much else can be impermanent.

The 'family' becomes a medium to link its members, whose links with one another may otherwise be very attenuated. A crisis will occur if any member of the family wishes to leave by getting the 'family' out of his system, or dissolving the 'family' in himself. Within the family, the 'family' may be felt as the whole world. To destroy the 'family' may be experienced as worse than murder or more selfish than suicide. 'It would be to destroy my parents' world' and felt as such by the parents. And what the parents do may be experienced by the children as shattering if it breaks up the 'family' as well as the family.

Dilemmas abound. If I do not destroy the 'family', the 'family' will destroy me. I cannot destroy the 'family' in myself without destroying 'it' in them. Feeling themselves endangered, will they destroy me?

Acts not so motivated or intended are defined *by the others* as destructive, or persecutory, or sick because they entail the breakup of their 'family'. Each must sacrifice himself therefore to preserve the 'family'.

The 'family' comes to serve as a defence or bulwark against total collapse, disintegration, emptiness, despair, guilt, and other terrors.

The preservation, change, or dissolution of the 'family' is not allowed to be a purely private affair when the 'family' has to be felt to be preserved by *all* its members. Loss of a family member may be less dangerous than a new addition to the family if the new recruit imports another 'family' into the 'family'.

Hence the preservation of the 'family' is equated with the preservation of self and world and the dissolution of the 'family' inside *another* is equated with death of self and world-collapse. Alternatively, one hates or fears the 'family', or envies others their happy or contented family life; the world will collapse if the 'family' is not assassinated.

Either way the shadow of the 'family' darkens one's vision. Until one can see the 'family' in oneself, one can see neither oneself nor any family clearly.

A GAME OF TENNIS

At the age of seventeen, Jane presented the appearance of early schizophrenia simplex. Active at school, with the usual quota of friends, keen on sports, especially tennis, over a period of several months she had become inactive, disinterested, and self-absorbed. When I saw her, she had become almost entirely motionless and silent. She would, however, allow herself to be dressed; she ate what was put in her mouth; and she complied passively with forceful pressures, but took no initiative, and, left to herself, she would do nothing.

She was absorbed in a reverie of a perpetual game of tennis. Mixed doubles. Centre Court. Wimbledon. The crowd, the court, the net, the players, and the ball, back and forth, back and forth, back and forth. She was all these elements, especially the ball.

This ball was served, smashed, volleyed, lobbed, sometimes hit right out of court – so small, so passive, yet so resilient – the centre of the game and spectacle. All eyes are on it. Though resilient, its endurance is limited. It can be worn out, though it began with a lot of bounce. It is the medium of the relationship between the players. They apply spin, trick and cheat with it. Although it is so essential, no one is really interested in it. They use it or want it only to beat the other side. Sometimes they treat it gently but only to win. No one cares about it. It is treated entirely ruthlessly. If the ball should protest or rebel, or not keep up with the beating it is taking, if it aspires to initiative, or option how to bounce, where to go, it will be thrown away. The game's the thing: not perhaps even fundamentally a matter of winning it, but of perpetuating it.

Suppose the ball metamorphosed. It might turn into a hand grenade and blow up the players. It might even turn into an atom bomb and blow up the whole Centre Court, the spectators, and half of London. It may be a time-bomb, set to go off just at some critical point, without itself knowing when or how.

What revenge! What a reversal! But if it explodes, it will be the first to be destroyed. Perhaps even the intolerable existence of a tennis ball, beaten, burning, parched, threadbare, covered in the hot and dry dust of the furnace of the Centre Court under the glare of the merciless sun, and subject to the indifferent stare of the spectators, is better than nothing.

Besides, this might be what she is. This might be her karma. She may have been a princess under an evil spell. Maybe she has to accept this as her fate, to forgo a happy destiny to expiate an unremembered crime, or as a sacrifice, as an example, or out of a mysterious spring of love.

The family set-up, under the one roof, consisted of father and mother, mother's father and father's mother, ranged against each other, father and his mother against mother and her father: mixed doubles. She was the ball in their game. To give one instance of the accuracy of this metaphor: the two sides would break off direct communication with each other, for weeks at a time, while communication was maintained through Jane. At table, they would not speak to each other directly. Mother would turn to Jane and say, 'Tell your father to pass the salt.' Jane would say to her father, 'Mum wants you to pass her the salt.' He would say to Jane, 'Tell her to get it herself.' Jane would say to her mother, 'Dad says to get it yourself.'

When Jane was a little girl her mother had a 'psychotic episode'.

Her mother then felt that the family was disconnected. Everyone had to sit round a table, silent, motionless, hands outstretched, palms down, with the tip of one person's thumb touching the fifth finger of his or her neighbour. Her mother prayed that a current of love would flow round the family circle to heal their distress. What a mad idea! They did it to humour her, but did not take it seriously. Might it work?

Jane had lost the link between her reverie of the game of tennis and the family . . . This link was the 'family'. One of the things not expected of a tennis ball is that it should know it is a tennis ball.

Jane saw the connections in three months, left the family two years later, and has been active in the world for ten years since.

The 'family' as fantasy may be 'unconscious'.[1]

Elements of the 'family' as a dramatic template surface to awareness clothed in different images. The 'family' undergoes modulations and other transformations in the process of internalization and in its subsequent history as fantasy.

The 'family' mapped onto the family, or carried over to other situations, is no simple set of introjected objects, but more a matrix for *dramas*, patterns of space-time sequences to be enacted. As in a *reel* of a film, all elements are co-present, pre-set to unfold in sequence in time as a *film* on the screen. *The reel is the internal family.*

[1] See Laing (1970) for discussion of the phenomenology of 'unconscious fantasy'.

The 'family' is not the only reel in a person, ready to unfold under suitable circumstances; nor necessarily the most significant for all. One is traversed by and one traverses innumerable sets of subsystems within the infinite totality of all sets that together compose the universe, and one occupies innumerable positions in these innumerable sets.[1]

The creation of the 'family' occurs in the first years of life. It entails internalization, understood here as experiential modulation and structural transformation. The internalization of a set of relations by each element of the set transforms the nature of the elements, their relations, and the set, into a group of a very special kind. This 'family' set of relations may be mapped onto one's body, feelings, thoughts, imaginations, dreams, perceptions; it may become scenarios enveloping one's actions, and it may be mapped onto any aspect of the cosmos. The whole cosmos may become mapped by a family scenario traceable to the prototypical 'family' set of relations and operations. This 'family' group prototype is transferred or carried over (*Übertragung:* carry-over) from one range[2] to another, remaining the domain from which projections are projected. Co-inherence compounded by reciprocal mapping of the 'family' of each onto the common family leads to what I have called the *nexification* of the family. Such nexified families may become relatively closed systems; they are seen again and again in studying families of people diagnosed schizophrenic. *This statement is very different from any assertion that such families cause schizophrenia.*[3]

[1] I do not imply that any of these remarks apply to more or other than appearances.

[2] For explanations of these terms, see 'Mapping', p. 117.

[3] See Preface to Second Edition of Laing and Esterson, *Sanity, Madness, and the Family* (1970).

In speaking of the family or the 'family' we are only beginning to glimpse what we may perhaps suppose we have been trying to describe.

Intervention in Social Situations[1]

The common ground between social workers and psychiatrists is the study of and intervention in social situations,

This is not all social workers or psychiatrists do, but it is something we are always doing, whatever else. When a doctor, in a purely medical capacity, diagnoses tonsillitis in a child, or cancer in an adult, and orders the child into hospital for tonsillectomy, or the parent into hospital for investigation and operation, he is intervening in a social situation to which he may have neither time nor interest to give more than passing notice. We hope family practitioners realize, and often they do, that 'purely' medical decisions have massive reverberations in a whole network of people, with consequences to many other than the patient alone. But in a medical emergency the person's physical health or even life precedes all else, and social reverberations generated by the emergency and medical intervention are, more often than not, left to reverberate away.

The child goes into hospital. It is difficult to keep track even of the individual, let alone the social consequences of such a momentous event. We should not require research workers to tell us there are profound repercussions in the family when a child or a parent is hospitalized. Hardly any psychiatrists, and too few social workers, fully realize the

[1] Lecture given at the Association of Family Caseworkers, May 1968.

extent of social resistances against admitting these repercussions. I refer to the U.K. primarily.

For some years I have been directly concerned with *the study of people in situations*. Usually I am 'called in' to a 'situation' which has already been defined by the people in it, and possibly also by other agents of society, as one in which there is 'something the matter' with *one* person in the situation; and the others do not know what to do about him or her; it is implied that if that one person were all right the situation would right itself. That is, I am called into a social crisis, defined as (regarded as due to, caused by, generated by, occasioned by, provoked by) a medical emergency.

There are many types of social crisis: when defined as a medical emergency, the view usually is that if the medical emergency is dealt with, that is, if the patient is treated adequately and recovers, then this will resolve the social crisis (provided this crisis has not generated another: e.g. an economic crisis). When a particular social situation is defined as a social crisis occasioned by a medical emergency, this definition is a call for a particular type of action: it is an unequivocal prescription to get one person right by 'treatment' and, if thought necessary, to give auxiliary help to the other members of the situation to cope with illness in the one person, and with its secondary social consequences. The definition of the situation and the call for action are two sides of the same coin. The correct rational strategy of intervention is prescribed in and through the definition of the situation.

Much of the area between social work, medicine, and psychiatry concerns such situations: the family of a retarded child, families where there is a physical disability in one person. In many cases, we talk about a *mental* disability (excluding subnormality and other clearly organic conditions) acute or chronic; we construe the situation in terms of the above schema, and act towards it in the way demanded by it.

Let us examine some of the practical consequences when this medical model of a social situation is adopted by social workers. Social workers and psychiatrists have to be practical. We have hectic jobs: our theorizing is often done in the midst of our activity, or in our spare time when we are not too exhausted. We often discover what we do after we have done it. An advantage of this is a certain empirical pragmatic approach. Disadvantages are that without time for critical reflection we may become dogmatic in theory, and keep repeating ourselves in practice. We may even keep repeating a story about what we repetitiously do that does not even match what we do: especially if we do not have sufficient time to scrutinize what we are actually doing. When what we think we do does not coincide with what we do do, we sink into assumptions that get pickled into our attitudes and we may find ourselves (if we ever find ourselves again) so pickled that we can longer see what our assumptions are, nor that we are perpetuating practices we do not recognize. Another danger is that we let others do the theorizing, while we do the work. None of us can afford to take on trust statements by people who think they can tell us what we are doing, or should be doing: people who do not actually do the practical work themselves, but who feel they are in a position to theorize about it. This is a dangerous state of affairs.

My impression is that much social work theory is based upon, or heavily influenced by, a medical model derived from psychiatry that psychiatry has itself derived from general medicine: that this psychiatric medical model has been taken, up until very recently at least, on trust even by psychiatrists. This model, when applied to a social situation, helps us to see what is going on about as much as do dark glasses in an already darkened room.

When I have been called into a situation usually one person has come to be regarded as having 'something the matter with' him or her; usually, 'expert' opinion has also begun to see something 'mentally' the matter with this one person. I will give you an example. You will understand it has to be curtailed and highly schematized.

THE CLARKS

A letter from a Child Guidance Clinic asks me to give an opinion on a nine-year-old boy who had been given a diagnosis at the clinic of ? incipient schizophrenia. He had been attending the clinic one afternoon each week for three months seeing a psychiatrist. His mother took him along to the clinic, and she has been having, once a fortnight, a talk with a psychiatric social worker. The boy has not improved; his behaviour at home and at school is deteriorating; his psychiatrist wonders why, because he is mute with him most of the time, and he thinks he might be developing schizophrenia. If this were presumed to be the case, things could be done, such as hospitalization to a child psychiatric unit. Because of restlessness in class, he had already been referred to a children's hospital, where, by lumbar punctures and other investigations, no 'organic pathology' had been discovered.

When I receive such a referral letter I have to decide not

only how to meet the person who is already the elected patient, but how to get the best glimpse in the shortest time of what is going on. This, already, is not what I have been asked. I was asked for a diagnosis. I have redefined my task. This is legitimate. Our client does not always define his terms as we would. We should not ignore his terms, but we are not bound to adopt them as ours, even when the client is a psychiatrist.

I could have arranged for mother and boy to come to see me. I could have gone to the clinic to see the boy alone or in a joint consultation with the psychiatrist. I could have done a number of things. What I did was to write asking his mother to telephone me. Over the telephone a visit to their home was arranged with two social therapists, in the early evening, when as many members as possible of the family would be present. We spent about two and a half hours with the nuclear family: the boy's mother, two elder brothers (13 and 11), his younger sister (7), and his father. In this period we saw Mr and Mrs Clark with the children; David alone; Mr and Mrs Clark alone. I was shown around the house and given details of the eating and sleeping and other arrangements of the family.

To pick up one or two bits. We met first in the sitting-room: mother, father, a brother of 13 years, a brother of 11 years, David aged 9, and sister aged 7. I asked Mrs Clark at one point:

'Who do your children take after?'

Pointing to her eldest son, she said:

'Well, that's his father sitting there.'

The second son does not take after anyone.

'Sister takes after David. That's part of the trouble, she is beginning to take after David.'

'Who does David take after?'

'*David takes after me.*'

'What is the matter with David, then?'

The matter with David (Mrs Clark rattles the list off) is that he is completely out of her control, he will not do what he is told, she can't get to the bottom of him, he stays out of the house, he won't tell her when he is coming back, he is not interested in reading or writing, and finally 'he's not worried'.

This in the first twenty minutes. Later she showed me around the house; where the boys slept, where the girl slept, where she and her husband slept, and so on. As we stood on the upstairs landing while the rest of the family were downstairs, I asked her:

'How did all this really start?'

'Well, he stays out all the time, he won't tell me when he is coming back, he just won't do what I tell him – he defies me. One afternoon when he was supposed to come back to lunch at 1 o'clock, and father was away and he hadn't come in by 2 o'clock – I said, "You've got to come in for your meals and you are going to do what I tell you." He said, "No, I won't," and I said, "Yes, you will. If you don't do what I tell you I will send you away" – "Go ahead".'

She did not know what to do. Hardly knowing what she was doing she phoned the police and said in front of him: 'I have a boy here who is out of my control. I don't know what to do with him.' They said 'Wait a minute.' She waited and waited (for two minutes) and then they came back on the phone and told her to take him to her local Child Guidance Clinic and gave her the address. This she did, and they have been going once a week to the local Child Guidance Clinic since then, for the last three months. She feels bad about it now, but David still will not do as he is told and he still does not seem to be worried.

After seeing Mrs Clark, I had a chat with David, both of us standing by the window in the boys' bedroom. It was a man-to-man chat in which he told me what he was doing – he was out with the workmen, helping them on a building site. He wasn't particularly interested in reading or writing but he was very interested in working with things. At the Child Guidance Clinic the only thing he enjoyed was draw-ing: they had his permission to use his paintings at an exhibi-tion of the children's art (another example perhaps of psychotic art?). But he said the main reason for going to the Child Guidance Clinic was a bad one because he got off school that afternoon: it did not pay because he had to make up on his lessons the following day. I asked if there was anything I could do for him. He asked me to arrange if possible for him not to go to the Child Guidance Clinic. I said I would see what I could do.

In the last forty minutes of the two and a half hours, we met Mrs Clark and Mr Clark without the children.

Mrs Clark had said that David took after her in those respects that the trouble seemed to be about.

Who did *she* take after in that case? She said, right away, 'My father.'

'In that case David takes after his grandfather.' She had not quite put it together like that, but with only a slight pause she said:

'Oh yes, of course, that's what my mother is always saying.'

Mother is an only daughter. Father is the younger of two brothers; his father (David's father's father) died when father was a boy. Father's mother is still alive. David's mother's father died just before David was conceived. David's father developed a close bond with his first son right away. They had another son. This was all right with Mrs Clark, but not with her mother-in-law. She had had two sons: her elder son had had two sons: now her second son had two sons. She wanted a grand-daughter. So Mrs Clark got pregnant again, to give her mother-in-law a present of a grand-daughter, just after her father died. As it was, she produced David, called after her father. Finally they tried a fourth time, and, thank god, she had a girl this time, who was immediately annexed by Mr Clark's mother.

Mrs Clark had taken after her father when she was David's age. He was an easy-going sort of chap, out of the house most of the time, doing what he shouldn't (according to her mother). He would never tell her what he was up to and who he was with, or why he would come in late. He was not very interested in making money, but made enough, and never learnt to read or write. Mrs Clark was very fond of her dad and took after him, but her mother beat that out of her and she became a good girl. Now she sees the same things 'coming out of' David. Her mother keeps on telling her that she should have beaten it out of David as had been done with her. But she couldn't bring herself to do so, and now it is too late. She sometimes feels that she likes him very much and maybe there's nothing the matter with him. She remembers what she felt like when she was his age.

From the foregoing it might be difficult to see why David should have begun to be seen as a possible schizophrenic. The 'schizophrenia' can be helped to come out more in the way the 'history' is inflected, and with skilful use of appropriate psychiatric schizophrenese. In class he was irritable, distractable, and restless (these are 'hypomanic' terms), but his mother's story that he was impossible, that she could not do anything with him, invites the term 'negativism'; he did not speak to the psychiatrist ('mutism'), he was cheerful when everyone was very worried ('inappropriate affect'): these are more schizophrenic terms. This is a game of earnest triviality. Such differential diagnosis of David is an elaborate diversion from the important issue: *to diagnose* (literally to see through) *the social situation*.

We can just glimpse in this family a drama perpetuated over three generations – the players are two women and a man: first, mother, daughter, and father; second, mother, daughter, and daughter's son. Daughter's father dies – daughter conceives a son, *to replace* her father. The play's the thing. The actors come and go. As they die, others are born. The new-born enters the part vacated by the newly dead. The system perpetuates itself over generations; the young are introduced to the parts that the dead once played. Hence the drama continues. The dramatic structure abides, subject to transformations whose laws we have not yet formulated and whose existence we have barely begun to fathom.

David is playing the part his grandfather once played. What will happen when he gets married? Marry his grandmother, produce his mother in his daughter, who will marry his father and produce him in his grandson? Who was his grandfather? *His* grandfather producing his grandson in himself? To talk in terms of identifications is misleading. It is shorthand for *b* plays the part *a* once played; grandson plays the part his grandfather played. The actors are *never* the parts they play (in this sense), even though they themselves may confusedly 'identify' themselves with their parts. The above, which I present to you in a very schematic abstract form, is all based on a type of everyday data open to any social worker and many others. It is based on the actual attributions made openly by people about people. It can be put on tape, reproduced, and studied completely objectively.

A very important area of the study of social situations is all that goes on beyond words: the *way* words are spoken (paralinguistics), the movements of people (kinesics). These data are equally objective, but at present not so easy to reproduce as words. So I have left them out. But none of this can be seen if one studies the situation in a fragmented way.

The case is typical – a psychiatrist had seen the boy, but no one else in the family. A psychiatric social worker had seen the mother, but not the boy or anyone else. The P.S.W. and the psychiatrist had seen each other at case conferences. No one had seen anyone else, or looked at the setting: no one had seen David's home, his school, the streets in which he played or, rather, worked. No one had reconstructed the situation. If we are not lulled by habit into regarding this as normal practice, is it not an odd way to go about things? If one has 'a referral', say, from a hockey team, because the left back is not playing properly, one wouldn't think only of getting the left back round to one's office, taking a history, and giving a Rorschach. At least I hope not. One would also go to see how the team plays hockey. One certainly would get nowhere if one had no idea of hockey, and what games within games can be played through it.

In our type of work no one knows in advance what the situation is. One has to discover it. When one element *of* the situation is a story told by some members of the situation *about* the situation to the effect that 'there is something the matter' with someone *in* the situation, this is already a tricky situation that merits careful investigation. They may be right. Someone may have pneumonia, a brain tumour, epilepsy, etc. It is for the doctor to diagnose and treat such a condition. They may be wrong. Many psychiatrists are still extraordinarily socially naïve. Most psychiatrists have never seen a whole family together, and, if they do, their medico-clinical model makes it more difficult for them than for an intelligent layman to see what is going on. When all the members of a situation start to define a situation as:

What is the matter with us all is that we have to cope with what is the matter with him (or her)

we must, first of all, put this manœuvre in brackets, *in* the situation as *we* see it. Whether or not there *was* anything the matter with an elected scapegoat to begin with, there soon will be if this process continues. It is one of the oldest-known social processes. In this case my report was that there was as yet nothing seriously the matter with this boy, but there soon would be (poor prognosis), in that if everyone continued to treat him as they were doing, he would be 'schizophrenic' in six months' time. I suggested that no one should see the boy if he did not wish to see anyone, but that someone should have sessions with Mrs Clark and her mother.

This situation is one of many that have the characteristic: *no one in the situation knows what the situation is.* If we stay in such a situation just a little, say for 90 minutes, we get more and more lost, confused, disorientated. People talk as though they knew what was going on; they have no idea, nor have we. They act as if they understood each other, when no one does. Not all situations are like this, though this is an important class of situation. The example I just gave can be regarded as a subtype of this class; a situation presented as a non-situation.

Consider the following situation:

Two parents are worried about their daughter of 16 because they think she has started to take drugs, is keeping bad company, and is not talking to them. They consult a clinic. A psychiatric social worker in the clinic takes a history from the parents. She consults the psychiatrist. In view of the history she has taken from the parents, an appointment is given to the girl to see the psychiatrist. She does not keep the appointment. She is given another. She turns up an hour late. The psychiatrist finds that her way of communicating to him is defective. He arranges to see the parents together. He tells them that his colleague, the P.S.W., has consulted with him, and he has now seen the girl and in his opinion she is seriously ill: she is likely to be psychotic in six months' time unless she comes off drugs: she has no insight into the harm she is doing herself. His recommendation (since she is without insight, is uncooperative, shows no desire to come off drugs, have psychotherapy, or give up her association with the bad company she is keeping) is that they should ask the powers-that-be to bring her before a juvenile court as being beyond their care, protection, and control.

The psychiatrist has not seen the parents with the girl. She had never heard of the fact that the parents had gone to the clinic until she got a letter from the psychiatrist 'giving' her an appointment. The P.S.W. has not seen the girl. No one has seen the whole family together. No one has ever dreamt of talking to her boyfriend, who comes around the house often. Might it not be civilized to talk the matter over with all concerned, including the boyfriend, before we start psychotherapizing anyone (a form of violence under certain circumstances only more subtle than bringing in the police)? I cannot give details of this situation, but I can say that, when it was eventually investigated as a situation, we found one 'real' issue to be between the girl's father and her boyfriend. They both 'smoked' less than average in their school. They were in fact, for their age, 'conservative': they took their stand on principle, as their parents had done on other matters in their time.

THE SITUATION HAS TO BE DISCOVERED

No one in the situation may know what the situation is. We can *never assume* that the people in the situation know what the situation is. A corollary to this is: *the situation has to be discovered*. You may think this is a banal proposition, but consider the implications. The stories people tell ('people' here includes all people, parents, children, fellow social workers, psychiatrists, ourselves) do not tell us simply and unambiguously what the situation is. These stories are part of the situation. There is no *a priori* reason to 'believe' a story, because anyone tells us it, as there is no *a priori* reason to disbelieve a story, because anyone tells it. One may have good reason, after putting it to the test, to trust certain people's stories. The stories we are told and tell are always significant parts of the situation to be discovered, but their truth value is often negligible.

This includes the stories that professional 'history'-takers tell. Imagine a psychiatric 'history' of Jesus. It is naïve to think one discovers a situation by taking a 'history' from one or two parties. But such a 'history' of the situation is *a sample of the situation*. What one does when 'taking a history' is not primarily to discover *history*. One uncovers a story, that is, one person's way of defining the situation; this way of defining the situation may be an important part of the situation *we* are trying to discover. Nor do dates make history. Dates are discontinuous markers left behind by history: dates are made by history. During our initial intervention, it may be very instructive to hear the stories people tell. Few psychiatrists are experts in sorting out these stories. They are experts in construing situations in terms of a few standard psychiatric myths.

Everyone has their stories as to why and what is happening. Often they agree – no more likely to be true thereby. There is no necessary or constant relationship between what people do, what they think they do, and what they say they are or have been doing.

When the situation has 'broken down' to the extent that an outside agency is brought in, not only may some or all of those in the situation not themselves see what the situation is, but also *they may not see that they do not see it.* To realize this may be *very* frightening for them, and is frightening enough for *us*, who are not 'in' it in the same way. If they can see they cannot see it, and begin to see it, we sometimes hope that thereby they will be better able to cope adequately themselves. But frequently, a contributing *cause* of the breakdown of the situation, as well as an effect of the breakdown (so it seems to us), is that the situation cannot itself be seen by any of the people in it for what we think we can see it to be. Any formulation of this type invites us to develop a social theory of *social ignorance and mystification*.

Our field of distinctive competence is the study and intervention into relatively small (micro) social situations: in no social situations can we *assume* that the participants know what the situation is; maybe some do – maybe they do not – we cannot take the definition of the situation as given us by the members of the situation as more than a story they tell, itself part of the situation we are to discover. We have to discover what the situation is *in the course of* our intervention in the situation. One way to discover what a situation is (so obvious, and yet frequently not done), is to convene in the one place, at the one time, the set of people we have good initial reason to suppose compose the key elements of the situation.

We require to formulate the possible and the most appropriate *strategies of intervention in situations*. Casework or psychotherapy with one person is one strategy of intervention *in that situation* of which that one person is a member.

We have hardly begun to list and to classify strategies of intervention, much less to think what may be best adapted to what situations. We have not even a systematic typology of situations in the first place, much less a classification of the ways one may intervene.

For instance: situations are presented to us, defined by the people in them in the following ways:

1. Something is the matter with someone.
2. Nothing is the matter with anyone, but nothing's working properly.
3. Something is the matter with everyone, according to everyone else.

In other situations we are called in where the people 'in' the situation, about which there is concern or complaint, say:

4. Nothing is the matter either with us or with the situation. Don't bother us, why are you interfering? Everything is fine as far as we are concerned. But it might not be fine as far as the police are concerned, or the neighbours.

By what criteria does who decide whose views are 'right'? Is this an inappropriate question? If we are already embarked on the perilous project of intervening somewhere, it is a different situation for us, whether the people in the situation say that there's nothing the matter with them or the situation, or that there is something the matter with one or two persons in the situation, or that there is nothing the matter with any of them but the *situation* is a mess. And so on.

I can do no more here and now than allude to the major task of finding adequate ways of formulating the problems implicit in the above.

Similarly, I can do no more than allude to the whole subject of the practical strategies of intervention open to us. The following example indicates that there are more forms of intervention than many of us have yet imagined.

This story is told by Gregory Bateson about a situation in Hawaii (unpublished). It is in his words.

'In a family with ten children there was a little boy, the fifth or sixth child, who had a long delinquent history: he was in and out of institutions; finally he landed in the hands of a particular psychiatric casework agency (the Lilinokalani Trust) who are Hawaians themselves.

They have an occidental psychiatrist who works with them and a young male social worker who went to see the mother of this boy, the father being dead. The social worker discovered that the history was related to a broken promise of the mother. When he learnt this related to a broken promise, the social worker wanted to drop the case at once. Hallucinating schizophrenics are one thing and everyone knows that this is psychiatry; but when you deal with broken promises ... The boy's behaviour seemed 'psychiatric' but the broken promise seemed to be something else. You deal with broken promises in Hawaii with ritual precautions. Something can rub off on you, because every promise contains a curse. You can't get a Hawaian to promise to come and do your gardening work on a Saturday for this reason, and in old Hawaii they did not make promises. However, the mother had made a promise to her mother, that is the grandmother of the patient, that she would never marry a divorced man – grandma had married a divorced man and it had turned out wrong, and she had her daughter promise not to marry one. Grandma died – the daughter married a divorced man, had ten children, and the middle one was now the patient.'

It is interesting, Bateson says, that in general this broken-up culture remembers what is wrong and how you get into religious and supernatural trouble, but it cannot remember the nature of the old cultural remedies. Perhaps we are further 'gone' than that. We cannot even 'diagnose' what is the matter any more.

'In old Hawaii the correct thing to do in the above circumstances is to have a "Ho'o Pono Pono". This is a gathering of the entire family, which may comprise several households of married siblings and offspring. In this meeting each member is asked to voice everything he has against every other member of the group. Having voiced all the complaints he can think of against members of the group, he is asked by the meeting's chairman (who is usually a priest or may be the family's head): "Do you disentangle him?"

To which he must reply: "Yes."

Then he is asked: "Who disentangles you?" Because the entanglement is mutual.

The correct answer is "God".'

'This,' says Bateson, 'may be a post-missionary addition to the ritual.'

'Obviously we can't start next Tuesday to get twenty or thirty people and have them mean this when asked, and they must answer and mean it. You must, therefore, devote from six months to three years to working on every member of this network to the point where they can come to this meeting and mean it. The final gathering of the whole group is in a sense a ritual affirmation of that which has been gone through over the six months or three or four year period. In this particular case they decided they would work towards a Ho'o Pono Pono and the members of the family started working on each other to plough up the ground.

From the moment they started to work on it the boy started to go straight. He is now doing very nicely at high school, getting good marks, and has been out of institutions for a couple of years. After some months they had what they regard as an abortive Ho'o Pono Pono. They could not get everyone to talk straight but they are working on it and are expecting in two or three years' time to have the real Ho'o Pono Pono. It's as sophisticated as anything we do, possibly more sophisticated than anything we can do.'[1]

[1] Speck's work in Philadelphia with networks is the most sophisticated I know. See Speck (1966).

DIFFERENCES BETWEEN SOCIAL AND MEDICAL
DIAGNOSIS

A few final remarks about social situations in relation to the medical model. Medical diagnosis finds its place in the context of a set of procedures in which all doctors are trained and which influences for life all who have been trained in them. Essentially it is this. When one comes to see anyone as a patient, one listens to the complaint, takes a history, does an examination, institutes whatever supplementary investigations one feels to be necessary, arrives at a diagnosis, makes a prognosis if one can, and having done all that, one prescribes treatment. Complaint, history, examination plus investigations, diagnosis, prognosis, treatment. Diagnosis includes aetiology, where aetiology is thought to be known. Often it implies prognosis. In all cases it determines treatment: no rational therapy without prior diagnosis: it is reckless and irresponsible to attempt to treat anyone without having arrived at, at least, a tentative diagnosis on the basis of which one's treatment is instituted.

Consider this model in relationship to the diagnosis of a social situation. One encounters a situation, defined in the first place by the people in it, and/or by agents in other situations. As soon as one is presented with any situation one is interacting with elements of it, and hence, willy-nilly intervening in one way or another. As soon as one intervenes, the situation changes somewhat, however little. A doctor does not usually feel he intervenes, in this sense, in the processes of, say, cardiovascular failure, or tuberculosis, simply by hearing the complaint, taking a history, doing an examination. He has not started to intervene with a view to *change* until he begins his treatment, *after* he has done all that is necessary to arrive at his diagnosis. In our case, we are intervening in and changing the situation *as soon as* we are involved. As soon as we interplay with the situation, we have already begun to intervene willy-nilly. Moreover, our intervention is already beginning to change *us*, as well as the situation. *A reciprocal relationship has begun.* The doctor and the still predominantly medically oriented psychiatrist use a non-reciprocal static model: history comes after the complaint; examination comes after the history; *after* this one makes a tentative or if possible *definitive* diagnosis; thereafter comes 'therapy'.

Diagnosis is *dia:* through; *gnosis:* knowledge of. *Diagnosis* is appropriate for social situations, if one understands it as *seeing through the social scene.* Diagnosis *begins* as soon as one encounters a particular situation, and never ends. The way one sees through the situation changes the situation. As soon as we convey in any way (by a gesture, a handshake, a cough, a smile, an inflection of our voice) what we see or think we see, *some* change is occurring even in the most rigid situation.

We may feel that one way to change most quickly, and radically, and *relevantly*, a situation is to take one or two of the people 'in' the situation 'out' of the situation, and 'give' them individual psycho-'therapy'. We engage in 'therapy' with a married couple, to get them to tell us how they see the situation, and to tell them what we think we can see, in the hope that this interchange will help to change the situation. It is naïve to expect that, by telling people what we think we see they are doing, we will enable them to stop doing it. Perhaps it is just as well that it is not so easy.

Social diagnosis is a process: not a single moment. It is not an element in an ordered set of before–after events in time.

In the medical model, such a sequence is the ideal, to which one tries to approximate in practice: complaint; history; examination; diagnosis; treatment. Intervention in social situations may have different phases: they overlap, contrapuntally. The phases cannot be chopped up into time-slices.

What one sees as one looks into the situation changes as one hears the story. In a year's time, after one has got to know the people and their situation a little, the story will have gone through a number of transformations: often it will be very different from what one heard a year back; neither version is necessarily untrue or true. It is a different story, or one *hears* a different story. As the story is transformed as time goes by, so what one sees undergoes transformations. At a particular time one is inclined to define the situation in a particular way; this definition in turn changes the situation in ways we may never be able to define. One's definition of the situation may generate different stories. People remember different things, put things together in different ways. This redefines the situation as changed by our definition in the light of how it originally presented itself to us. Our definition is an act of intervention that changes the situation, which thus requires redefining; it introduces a new factor. At any moment of time, in the continuous process of looking through, of diagnosis, we see it in a particular way that leads us to a nondefinitive definition, subject to revision in the light of the transformations that this very definition induces, prospectively and retrospectively. Medically, our diagnosis does not affect the fact that the person has tuberculosis. We do not change the illness by our diagnosis. You do not convert a case of tuberculosis into a cardiac failure by calling it cardiac failure. But suppose our diagnosis of a situation is: This is a social crisis, *due to the fact* that this boy has 'got' schizophrenia. We must treat the 'schizophrenia' in the boy, and the social worker must help the relatives to cope with the terrible tragedy of having a mental illness in the family and so forth. This is not merely a medical diagnosis. It is a social prescription. As you know, in my view, it is a gross misreading of the situation. In any event, whether you agree with me or not, there is no doubt that any such medical diagnosis also defines and changes the situation. Such a definition may even be an 'aetiological factor' in creating the situation one has defined: even in creating the 'illness' one is purporting to cure. Social situations are *the* field for the self-fulfilling prophecy. A self-fulfilling diagnosis of the situation tends to induce a situation as defined.

One must not be *naïve*. Who are the experts in such matters? Not many psychiatrists at present. Most have no training whatever in this respect, and have often been trained to be incompetent in this regard.

We all must continually learn to unlearn much that we have learned, and learn to learn that we have not been taught. Only thus do we and our subject grow.

The Study of Family
and Social Contexts in Relation to
'Schizophrenia'[1]

I

In addressing ourselves to the problem of the origins of schizophrenia, it would be helpful if we could agree about what schizophrenia *is*. But a scrutiny of the papers presented at this Congress alone leaves doubt whether we do agree about what it is whose origins we are seeking.

I am unhappy about using the term schizophrenia at all. But it would be somewhat whimsical to eliminate it from my vocabulary, since it is on the lips of so many.

Most, perhaps all of the speakers seem to give explicit or tacit assent to what I take to be an assumption: namely, that 'schizophrenia' is a condition that afflicts people diagnosed as schizophrenic. Their view appears to be that people are diagnosed as schizophrenic *because* they suffer from schizophrenia. The problem of the origins of schizophrenia is then to find out why some people and not others suffer from this condition.

There are a number of difficulties to this position. Whether

[1] Revised version of a paper published in 'The Origins of Schizophrenia: Proceedings of the First Rochester International Congress' (March 1967), *Excerpta Medica International Congress Series* No. 151.

one regards the condition that schizophrenics suffer from as organic, social, psychological, genetic, chemico-molecular, psychobiologico-social, I think it is a fair generalization that while, on the one hand, there is almost total agreement that there is a pathological condition called schizophrenia from which schizophrenics suffer, on the other hand, there is little agreement as to what this condition is. Every conceivable type of condition, from hereditary–organic to social–functional, together with every conceivable mix of them all, is proposed to define it.

In the face of the above, I propose to take a step back, and start from the following. *Schizophrenia is the name for a condition that most psychiatrists ascribe to patients they call schizophrenic.* This ascription is a system of attributions that has a variable internal consistency, and is predominantly derogatory. It is frequently in a mixture of clinical–medical–biological–psychoanalytical psychiatrese, which vies with schizophrenese itself in its apparent profound confusion.

Those who employ the term schizophrenia as a name for a pathological condition in some people fall into a self-validating explanation of why they do so, if they reason that they employ this term for a pathological condition, from which the patient suffers, *because* the patient is obviously suffering from a pathological condition whatever it may be. The pathological condition is either an assumption or a hypothesis. It cannot at present be taken as a fact because no one has so far discovered it. I am not making the assumption, nor pursuing that hypothesis. (I cannot deny the fact since there is as yet no fact to deny.)

This suggests research into the origins of schizophrenia is hunting a hare whose tracks are in the mind of the hunters. Under what circumstances is the ascription of schizophrenia brought into play? Why, and how, is its application perpetuated, by whom to whom, under what conditions?[1] What interpersonal and group functions does it serve? What would happen if this set of attributions was dropped?

A peculiar type of disjunction between two human beings, one a psychiatrist and the other a patient, is the final occasion, though not the origin, of the attribution of schizophrenia. To a much greater extent than most of us suppose, it may be that it is very largely the institutionalization of this attribution in a set of organized behaviours on the part of psychiatrists, mental nurses, social workers, family members, and others that *induces* much of the more consistently described subsequent behaviours of both acute and chronic schizophrenia, which tend to confirm the initial diagnosis in many cases.[2]

Research into the origin of schizophrenia requires that we begin at the beginning: that we put all presuppositions in brackets, and consider what is that whole long expanding spiral of multiple intensifying disjunctions, and *reciprocally* widening alienation, whereby one human being eventually puts a thermometer into another human being's mouth and anus in order to get data to account for the other person's extraordinary behaviour. It has taken more than one set of lifetimes to arrive at the situation described by Dr Shakow at this conference: one man asks another to take seven from a hundred, who replies: 'I don't believe in doing things

[1] See Laing and Esterson (1964).

[2] For a background to the sociology of deviance in relation to the ascription of mental illness, see Scheff (1967). Also Goffman (1961). Foucault (1965) places the development of the notion of mental illness in the perspective of European socio-economic and cultural history. Also, Szasz (1961), of course.

backwards.' In so saying, the latter (patient) confirms the former (psychologist) in the diagnosis already reached by the former's psychiatric colleagues.

We have only begun to scratch the surface of the origins of this particular system of attributions of disease to one member of a social system. Not only must we ask how and why in certain social circumstances is it expedient, even apparently unavoidable, to regard one member of a social network as subject to a disease called schizophrenia, but also: to what extent does behaviour diagnosed as schizophrenic become more intelligible when placed in the context of the original social situation where it belongs?

This does not mean that the behaviour of the person who is about to be diagnosed as suffering from this condition has nothing to do with the aetiology of schizophrenia. One might say that his or her behaviour, which induces the attribution, is one of the many aetiological factors in the genesis of schizophrenia. His behaviour is one of the 'causes' of 'schizophrenia'. But the endless spiral of social transaction has not begun and does not end there.

We are addressing the next movement of the spiral when we ask: to what extent does 'schizophrenia' 'cause' his subsequent behaviour? If you like: to what extent is the behaviour most typically regarded as hard-core schizophrenia, iatrogenic?

Hypothesis: this set of ascriptions to a person, and this induction into the role of schizophrenic, themselves generate much of the behaviour that is classified as 'symptomatology' of schizophrenia.

Experiment: Take a group of normal persons, group N (by agreed criteria)

Treat them as schizophrenic

Take a group of 'early' schizophrenics, group X (by agreed criteria)

Treat them as normal

Prediction: Many of N will begin to display the agreed criteria of schizophrenia

Many of X will begin to display the agreed criteria of normality

Experiment: Take a group of 'early' schizophrenics

    (i) treat them in role as crazy

    (ii) treat them like oneself as sane

Prediction: In (i) the 'symptomatology' of schizophrenia will be very much greater

    (ii) the symptomatology of schizophrenia will be greatly diminished

An experiment of such a kind is feasible, and as far as I know has not been done. How extraodinary.[1] However, informally, the 'predictions' above are the *post*dictions of my experience in the last twenty years in this field, shared by many others.

It is going to be difficult to study the *origins* of schizophrenia, if our research is restricted to situations where the attribution of schizophrenia and all that goes with it has already happened.

II

There are at least three key problems: sampling; context; and method. Each deserves an extended discussion in its own right. In what follows, I shall merely allude to some issues in

[1] For one such experiment, see Zarlock (1966).

the course of listing some of the research directions we have been pursuing in London. In the final section I shall revert to the individual, in the *light* however of our studies of social contexts, and put forward two fragments of theory towards understanding what is going on.

We have tried to sample behaviour by *a study of multiple social contexts*, by a method of social phenomenology.

1. Extensions of family studies

We have tried to see how far the diagnosed schizophrenic is as much an intelligible part of his family context as are the others who compose it. The emphasis has not so much been on developing a typology of family structures as on de-mystifying what we have always found to be highly mystified situations.[1] We have compared such situations with what goes on in 'normal' families.

Everyone who has made a close study of the families of schizophrenics appears to agree that much, or even all, of the apparent irrationality of the individual finds its rationality in its original family context. The family as a whole now appears irrational. Does the irrationality of the family will find *its* rationality when placed in *its* context? And so on . . . presumably through meta-meta-meta- . . . contexts, until one arrives at the context of all social contexts, the *Total World System* (TWS). This seems irrational enough, but may find its rationality in a further meta context of which we have only vague intimations.

Be that as it may, we have got as far as the study not only of *intra*familial operations, but also of *inter*family relations,

[1] See Laing and Esterson (1964); Laing (1965); Esterson (1970).

and interaction across family boundaries with extrafamilial networks. Speck in Philadelphia has recently carried this work further than anyone (as far as I know) at present.[1] He reported a remarkable case of a life-long mother–son (aged 20) symbiosis (father died shortly after son's birth, no brothers or sisters), where mother and son both had almost no contacts with anyone apart from the other. Speck's strategy was to reconvene the network out of which mother had dropped in the past 20 years, eventually bringing together at one meeting upwards of 35 people, representing elements from no less than seven nuclear families. He did not 'treat' the son or the mother individually, or as a dyad, but 'treated' the whole network. Extensive and intensive changes reverberated throughout the network, and among these were the break-up of the symbiosis between mother and son as both became involved for the first time in twenty years in collateral relationships in the network.

We have been led also to study what one might call *micro-history*–transformations extending to several generations in small social networks, especially families. This terrain lies between individual biography and larger-scale history. It is an area curiously neglected by sociologists, anthropologists, and historians.

2. The 'anti-hospital'

Dr David Cooper was responsible for the development at Shenley Hospital of what he called an 'Anti-Hospital' in one of the villas of the hospital that accommodated about twenty young male schizophrenics. He has given an account[2]

---

[1] See Speck (1966).
[2] Cooper (1967).

of part of this experiment, which ended in 1966. Briefly, in this subculture, as staff–patient role distinctions became blurred, Villa 21 became more of a household, without 'staff' putting 'patients' to bed, getting them up, drugging them, and so on. It became no longer clear who, if anyone, was 'treating' whom for what, since it was no longer discernible, or even an issue, who was sane and who was crazy.

3. The study of autobiographies and lives

More people than we perhaps realize go through experiences that would not be allowed to unfold if they were to consult psychiatrists about them. Bateson has drawn attention to such an account of special theoretical interest.[1] We have a growing number of protocols as yet unpublished by people who have managed to go through all sorts of transformations without hindrance.

4. Households

Since 1964 households have been operative in London[2] run by those who stay in them. Over one hundred and fifty people have stayed at these places. There are no staff and no patients, no one is a psychiatrist and no one is a schizophrenic. This experiment (currently on-going) has shown conclusively that many who behave in typically schizophrenic ways in some places behave differently in these households. What unfolds there is both more mundane than many

[1] See Bateson (1961).
[2] See Appendix to this chapter.

expected, and, in other respects, strange and new. In both directions, even the most liberalized mental hospital restricts the 'contingency possibilities' open to staff and patients alike. In these households there are rules, there is no rule against rules, but there is a rule that rules are open to examination and revision. Some of the people there, who have grown up in family systems with really fancy sets of rules, are expert at ferreting out concealed metarules, once in a place where they discover this activity is appreciated.

III

One may be high or low, beside oneself, move forwards, get further out or in, move in circles, go back, or stand still. Of these movements, the last two in particular tend to earn the attribution of schizophrenia. Perhaps the most tabooed movement of all is to go back (regression), and despite all that has been written about it, in my view it is still very little understood.

At Cooper's Villa 21 and in our households, this movement has not been stopped. If allowed to go on, a process unfolds that appears to be a natural sequence, with a beginning, middle, and end. Instead of the pathological connotations around such terms as 'acute schizophrenic breakdown', I shall for the moment simply designate this hypothesized sequence as X.

Looking back on it, people who have been through it often describe the X experience as a movement in, down, back, turning at the nadir, and then out up, forward into the world.[1]

I have never seen this X sequence get more than started

[1] See Laing (1972a).

within a family, and very seldom within a mental hospital. In our households I have seen this sequence run a course to end in what psychiatrists would call recovery, without drugs, electroshocks, or psychotherapy of a formal kind, and last from a few hours to over a year's incursion through archetypic forms, with many vicissitudes. It appears to be a sort of death–rebirth sequence, from which, if it is successfully negotiated, the person returns to the world feeling new-born, refreshed, and reintegrated at a higher level of functioning than before. I have given accounts of this voyage elsewhere,[1] though nowhere as yet more than sketches.

Paradoxically, many people diagnosed as schizophrenic are unable to make this voyage, either because they are prevented by treatment or because they are stuck. They are deeply immobilized in a complex knot, both internal and external, of contradictory, paradoxical attributions and injunctions. These people are often moved from the miserable, mystifying context of their families to the equally miserable and no less mystifying context of the mental hospital, without any existential change occurring.[2] Their families *and* the hospital both *prevent* them embarking on the X-route as a possible way out of their intricate entanglement. The beginning of the X-process may be feared by all, including the patient. *It is often regarded as the beginning of a schizophrenic illness, whereas it is the possible beginning of becoming well.* It is treated by tranquillization, cold packs, electroshocks, etc. If this X-process is confirmed by others to be what I suspect it to be, a healing resource sometimes open to just those people whose treatment consists in denying

[1] See Laing (1967a).
[2] See Haley (1965).

them this possibility, there is a tragic and ironical misunder-
standing.

In this section I shall sketch something of the *knot* one young
man of twenty-three was in when I first saw him. I present
this as a paradigm of the internalization of a multi-genera-
tional family situation, such as I have seen in a number of
people, and still leads to a diagnosis of schizophrenia. I shall
simplify enormously.

He experiences himself as follows:

Right side: masculine
Left side: feminine
Left side younger than right side.
The two sides do not meet.
Both sides are rotten, and he is rotting away with them to
an early death.

From psychoanalysis and other information:

His mother and father separated when he was five.
His mother told him he 'took after' his father.
His father told him he 'took after' his mother.
His mother said his father was not a real man.
His father said his mother was not a real woman.
To Paul, they were both right.
Consequently, on the one hand (or, as he would say, on
his right side), he was a female male homosexual, and on
the other hand (his left side), he was a male lesbian.
His mother's father (MF) died shortly after Paul was born.
Paul's mother said he took after her father.
But the issue of real or not-real had been reverberating
in this family for several generations.

His mother's mother (MM) did not regard her husband (MF) as a real man.

Nor did his mother's father (MF) regard his wife (MM) as a real woman.

Through the mediation of his mother, Paul thought that her father (Paul's grandfather) was identified with his mother's (Paul's great-grandmother's) identification with her father's (Paul's great-great-grandfather's) relation to his wife (Paul's great-great-grandmother).

Through the mediation of his father, Paul thought that his father's father was identified with his mother's (Paul's great-grandmother's) identification with her father's (Paul's great-great-grandfather's) ideal wife.

When we make a serious attempt to think *into* a three-generational family set, the situation becomes almost unbearably complex.

The *alterations*[1] of family identity alone are formidable. For instance: consider a man and woman, Jack and Jill. Jack is husband, father, grandfather, son. Jill is wife, mother, grandmother, daughter. If they have a son, who marries and has a daughter, Jill is eventually granddaughter, daughter, sister, wife, mother, grandmother, niece, cousin, etc., etc.

In a family, people can be designated by a name, Jill; by pronominal alterations, she, I, you, etc.; or by familial alterations, daughter, wife, mother, mother-in-law, grandmother. These *familial alterations* are the others Jill is to this or that or those others, or to herself. For her total familial existence to be feasible, these alterations must constitute a *compossible set*.

[1] Alteration: the process whereby self becomes other-to-other.

A person is, in one sense, a set of relations, and relations of and to relations.

Bill relates as son to his father. But who or what is his father? That man, Tom, he calls father is himself a set of relationships. So Bill (son), relating to Tom (father), is relating not only to Tom's relationship to Bill, but also to many other relationships.

$$\text{Son (Bill)} \rightarrow \text{F (Tom)} \begin{cases} \rightarrow \text{S (Bill)} \\ \rightarrow \text{M} \\ \rightarrow \text{pgrM (paternal grandmother)} \\ \rightarrow \text{pgrF (paternal grandfather)} \\ \rightarrow \text{(pgrM} \longleftrightarrow \text{pgrF)} \\ \rightarrow \text{etc.} \end{cases}$$

In addition, Bill (son) relates to Tom's (father's) relationship to his (Bill's) relationships. For instance: Bill may be made very much aware of how father (Tom) relates to Bill's (son's) relation to father's (Tom's) relation to Jean (Bill's mother, Tom's wife).

That is: S's relation to F's relation to S's relation to F's relation to M

$$S \rightarrow F \rightarrow S \rightarrow (F \longleftrightarrow M)$$

If M (Jean), let us say, disagrees with how F relates to S's relation to FM or MF, then S may be involved in

$$S \rightarrow M \rightarrow F \rightarrow S \rightarrow (F \longleftrightarrow M)$$

And family disjunction may, among other things, revolve around different views that S, F, and M have of $M \rightarrow F \rightarrow S \rightarrow (F \longleftrightarrow M)$

$$\text{e.g.} \quad S \rightarrow (M \rightarrow (F \rightarrow (S \rightarrow (F \longleftrightarrow M))))$$
$$\neq M \rightarrow (M \rightarrow (F \rightarrow (S \rightarrow (F \longleftrightarrow M))))$$
$$\neq F \rightarrow (M \rightarrow (F \rightarrow (S \rightarrow (F \longleftrightarrow M))))[1]$$

[1] Where $\neq$ means: not equivalent to.

to take only a very simplified fragment of a very simple instance.

Let us consider A's relation to himself. There is A's relation to himself as a son, and A's relation to himself as a father. Consider the relation between A's relation to himself in relation to his father and his father's relation to him, and A's relation to himself in relation to his relation to his son and his son's relation to him.

Each person's relation to himself is mediated through the relations between the relations that comprise the set of relations he has with others.

One step further. We have A's relation to his father and A's relation to his mother. A's relation to his father's relation to him. A's relation to his mother's relation to him. A's relation to his mother's relation to his father. A's relation to his father's relation to his mother. Also A's relation to his father's relation to his relation to the relationship between his father and mother. How A relates to *his* son's relation to A's relation to his wife, is related to how A related to how his father related to A's relation to his father's relation to A's mother.

To return to Paul. His mother thought she could be a better husband and father than his father. And his father thought he could be a better wife and mother than his mother.

In his view of his mother's view of her father, and his mother's view of her mother's view of *her* husband; and his father's view of his mother, and his father's view of his father's view of *his* wife, there had never been a real man or woman in the family for four generations.

Paul, through his internalization of this tangled set of relations of relations of relations, is tied in a knot, whereby he is effectively immobilized.

To summarize: on his right side he takes after father's view of him as taking after his mother, an unreal woman and phoney man. And on his left side he takes after his mother's view of him as taking after his father, an unreal man and phoney woman. But also, on his right side he identifies himself with his view of his father, and on his left side he identifies himself with his view of his mother. On his right side, moreover, he identifies himself with his mother's identification of him as *her* mother's ideal husband and father; and on his left side he identifies himself with his father's identification of him as *his* father's ideal wife and mother.

His body was a sort of mausoleum, a haunted graveyard in which the ghosts of several generations still walked, while their physical remains rotted away. This family had buried their dead *in each other*. The foregoing is a very simplified sketch of a complex process of the increasingly tortured and tortuous sexual confusion that had developed within the family structure, which we cannot go into here.

This young man was tied in a knot; it had taken at least four, perhaps five or more, generations to tie it.

CONCLUSIONS

The concept of schizophrenia is a straitjacket that restricts psychiatrists and patients. By taking off this straitjacket we can see what happens. It has been shown, in the field of ethology, that observations on the behaviour of animals in captivity tell us *nothing reliable* about their behaviour in their natural setting. The whole of our present civilization may be a captivity. But the observations upon which psychiatrists and psychologists have drawn in order to build up the prevailing picture of schizophrenia have, almost entirely, been made on human beings in double or even treble captivity.

Man does not always need bars for cages. Ideas can be cages too. Doors are being opened in mental hospitals as chemical constraints become more effective. The doors in our minds are the most difficult to open.

Marx said: under all circumstances a Negro has a black skin but only under certain socio-economic conditions is he a slave. Under all circumstances a man may get stuck, lose himself, and have to turn round and go back a long way to find himself again. Only under certain socio-economic conditions will he suffer from schizophrenia.

Part II
The Politics of the Family

Introduction

In these talks[1] I have sketched tentative outlines of some components of a prospective systematic theory that does not yet exist.

I have not presupposed in the listener or reader any knowledge of the work with families (therapy, research, theory) carried out, especially in the United States, in the last twenty-five years.

A list of the key people in this field, were it to include everyone, would be too long: and misleading, were I to mention the few who have especially influenced me. I have been influenced by some, primarily through their writings; others, by personal association and friendship; others indirectly, through their influences on others, etc. The reader new to this field, who wishes to follow through into the background of family studies of the kind from which these talks derive, can do so by looking up the footnoted references which, containing extensive bibliographies, are gate-openers to the whole field.

I hope that my fellow 'professionals' will find something to interest them here. The theory of sets and mapping is

[1] The following chapters are revised versions of five radio talks broadcast by the Canadian Broadcasting Corporation during November and December of 1968, as the eighth annual series of Massey Lectures. *The Politics of the Family* was originally published in book form by CBC Publications, 1969.

being applied to great effect in linguistics, kinship systems, mythology, and other areas of social science. Can we apply this way of thinking to the 'psychosocial interior' of families in our own society? Definitely yes. But what will it yield? Will it be fruitful, will it enable us to discover more, see more clearly, understand better, provide useful and effective guidelines for therapy, help to get our research designs into sharper outline? We do not yet know. This might be a treacherous cul-de-sac. But I think the risk is worth taking. It may be a way out of the cul-de-sac in which, *especially*, some of the technically best research in this field can get stuck. Careful, and meticulous, such research yet sometimes leads to a type of analysis of familial interactions that returns findings that can never answer the questions we really want answered. We have taught ourselves that it is useless to ask questions when we have no methodology to answer them. But, between the impossible and the trivial, there may be a way that is both feasible and significant. At any rate, I would like to be counted as still trying to find it.

I did not make it easy for the Canadian Broadcasting Corporation in preparing these talks. It is a pleasure to thank Phyllis Webb and Jeff Anderson of the CBC for making everything as easy as possible for me at all times.

R. D. Laing

London, January 1969

The Family and Invalidation

The first family to interest me was my own. I still know less about it than I know about many other families. This is typical. Children are the last to be told what 'really' was going on before they came into the world, especially when they want to know not merely a few discontinuous points in time, so-called 'dates', and other apparently 'hard' facts, such as who was born when, married whom, and died when and where, had what children when, earned what how, and so forth.

What is the texture of the actual lived experience of family life? How is the texture of this experience related to dramatic structure, the social *product* of the interweaving of many lives over many generations? Questions difficult to answer, since this dramatic structure, while a *product* of behaviour and experience, is as a rule unknown to the very people who generate and perpetuate it.

In this type of inquiry the dates of public family events do not take us far. We must neither ignore nor be deceived by them. Jack and Jill were married in 1960. There were over 100 wedding guests. Nevertheless Jack has never *felt* married to Jill, and Jill began to feel 'really' married to Jack only some months after the wedding.

Jack 'knows' he is married because he can remember a ceremony called a 'marriage', and he has over 100 witnesses to prove it. But Jill is not satisfied. She does not want a pretence of a marriage, a shell of a husband, a façade of a family. One night she started to say in front of the children that he wasn't a real husband. That she was married to him, but he wasn't married to her. He became upset, and phoned the doctor the next morning. People are sent to psychiatrists, and into hospitals, if they persist in such statements.

Jill's mother had a stroke in 1963. She recovered to live on, nursed by Jill, until she died two years later. Jill said her mother had died in 1963. She did not recognize her mother in the woman she nursed for two years. When her mother 'officially' died in 1965, she felt relief not grief.

Thus official dates of public events can be out of phase with the structure of experience. If we deny official definitions of public events, we are regarded as mad. A woman who says (and seems to mean it) her mother is dead, when she is alive, and her husband is not her husband, is regarded as psychotic.

Call experiential structure A, and public event B. Sometimes the product of A and B, in a marriage ceremony, is a Marriage. Both people are married in all senses at once. How often this happens I do not know.

One function of ritual is to map A onto B, at critical moments, for example births, marriages, deaths. In our society many of the old rituals have lost much of their power. New ones have not arisen.

A and B float, unattached, so that it is difficult to see what laws govern their relationship.

To preserve convention, there is general collusion to disavow A when A and B do not match. Anyone breaking this rule is liable to invalidation. One is not supposed to feel married if one has not been married. Conversely, one is supposed to feel married if one 'is'. If one goes through a marriage ceremony, and does not feel it is 'real', if it did not 'take', there are relatives and friends to say: 'Don't worry, I felt the same, my dear. Wait until you have a child . . . Then you will feel you are a mother,' and so on. It is more serious if one experiences the marriage ceremony as an *execution*: one is mapping A onto B in a way that is interdicted. So one feels, perhaps, frightened or guilty, and probably wishes to disavow A; to take refuge in B, where everything is as everyone says.

In this latter case, the set of elements comprising the structure of events as experienced not only must be privately *disavowed*, but must be *excommunicated*.

Conventions are convenient. It is inconvenient to say people are dead when they are alive, or alive when they have been buried, or that the world is crumbling when it is, as everyone can see, there as usual. If all A that does not fit B is *ipso facto* disqualified, we have to tailor A to shape and size to avoid serious trouble, and not all are equally gifted in this art.

Later I shall allude to some *operations* we do on our experience to legitimize it, to conform it to 'laws', often unwritten, unspoken, and unavowed.

When this system breaks down, a psychiatrist is liable to be called in – a strategy developed in Europe and North America recently, in the last 150 years.

Here is an account by Professor Morel, a French psychiatrist, of his intervention into a family, from his textbook of psychiatry, published 1860. It is of historical interest for the introduction of the term *dementia praecox*, a term still in use though generally superseded by the notion of 'schizophrenia'.

To Morel, dementia praecox was an insidious, inherited,

constitutional disease that comes over some young people, leading to a dementia. In a chapter on inherited taints and degeneracies, he writes:[1]

. . . I recall with sorrow a disorder of heredity of a progressive form which appeared in a family with whose members I grew up in my youth. An unhappy father consulted me one day on the mental state of his son, aged 13 or 14, in whom a violent hatred for the author of his being had suddenly replaced the most tender sentiments. When I first saw the child, whose head was well formed and whose intellectual faculties surpassed those of many of his school-fellows, I was struck by the fact that his growth had been arrested in some way. His chief miseries were related to this apparently futile source, which had nothing to do with peculiar anomalies of his feelings. He was in despair because he was the smallest of his class, although he always came first in 'composition' without any effort and almost without working. It was, so to speak, by intuition that he understood things and that everything classified itself in his memory and intellect. Gradually he lost his gaiety, became sombre, taciturn, and showed a tendency to solitariness. One would have thought that he had onanistic tendencies, but it was not so. The child's statement of melancholy depression and his hatred of his father, which was carried to the length of thinking of killing him, had a different cause. His mother was deranged, alienated, and his grandmother eccentric in the extreme.

I ordered that this child's studies be interrupted and he be isolated in an hydrotherapeutic institution. Gymnastic

[1] Morel (1860, p. 565).

exercises, baths, manual work, were to enter into the new health-conditions of his existence. These methods were pursued consistently and intelligently by a doctor as knowledgeable as he was enlightened (Dr Gillebert d'Hercourt), and a most happy modification was achieved in the organic state of the child. He grew considerably but the situation came to be dominated by another phenomenon just as worrying as those I have already spoken of. The young invalid progressively forgot all that he had learned; his brilliant intellectual faculties underwent a most worrying period of arrest. A kind of torpor akin to stupefaction replaced his former activity, and when I saw him again I judged that the fatal transition to that state of dementia praecox was in course of operation. This despairing prognosis is generally far from the minds of the parents, and even of the doctors who attend these children.

This, nevertheless, is in many cases the mournful end of hereditary madness. A sudden paralysis of all the faculties, a dementia praecox, indicate that the young subject has reached the end of the intellectual life he can expect.

This elegant, concise clinical description is the prototype for what must be millions of comparable diagnoses under comparable circumstances in the last 100 years.

With inessential changes, the *structure* in this presentation is still the *paradigm* of most clinical psychiatric examination, diagnoses, and treatment of a 'case'.

The presenting complaint is by an 'unhappy father' of a family Morel knew well. The complaint is that the son (aged 13 or 14) had 'suddenly' evidenced to the father 'a violent hatred' of him; whereas before, his father had had the impression that his son held 'the most tender sentiments' towards him. Morel's first comment *on the situation* is exclusively about the boy, not even about the whole boy: his head was well formed and intellectually he was above average. However, he was smaller than average. Such is the spell Morel casts, we may already regard this information as beginning to confirm a diagnosis the great clinician will lead us towards step by step by a process of exclusion, as a detective leads us to a criminal. Clearly there is nothing the matter with the father. That goes without saying. If the boy, according to the father, hates him, there *must* be something the matter with the boy. His head *looks* all right, and he is doing well at school. But he is rather short. Aha! . . . an arrest of development of an inherited constitutional nature. His chief source of misery appears to be that he is small. Aha! This has nothing to do with what is *really* the matter with him, namely, the fact that he hates his father. He has lost his gaiety, he has become sombre, taciturn, and shows a tendency to solitariness: a picture takes shape. Indeed, a new psychiatric syndrome is about to be invented. Sudden onset; the affects attacked first; evidence of a constitutional arrest of development . . . *must* be inherited. To clinch it, it does not appear to be caused by onanism (masturbation). And his mother and his grandmother showed signs of mental disorder. There is no question about it. He needs *treatment*. Immediately.

One hopes for the best, though one fears the worst. We must take him from school and isolate him in an 'hydro-therapeutic institution'. This will surely stop him hating his father. He grows a bit more. But unfortunately he does not 'respond' in other ways. Still, we can tell his father that we did all that could be done to get his son to love him. He has lost all interest in his studies, and will not speak to anyone now. But, look at his mother and grandmother. In those cases, when it is inherited, we are fighting a losing battle. We have to tell you that the chances of recovery are small.

This story is still all too common. Instead of dementia praecox, read process schizophrenia. Instead of 'hydrotherapeutic institution', read any one of our 'best' hospitals or sanatoria. Instead of 'gymnastic exercises, etc.', read group therapy, occupational therapy, milieu therapy. Add a touch of psychotherapy, a sprinkling of electroshocks for the depression, a dab of hormones for the arrest in his development, and some vitamins and drugs, so as not to deprive him of the benefit of any chance that recent advances in psychiatry can offer . . .

Why does he hate his father and why had he even thought of killing him? We shall never know.

The direct effect, and intention, of psychiatric intervention is to turn this young man into a 'young invalid': to *invalidate* his hatred of his father, under the name of treatment. In a minority of cases, 100 years ago, this treatment worked. Such young persons would decide *not* to hate their fathers, that is, not to exhibit the 'signs' of the 'illness' for which they were receiving such 'treatment'. A few might even learn to be grateful. Perhaps psychiatry today is more *effective*. In a greater percentage, remission of symptoms and lower relapse rates are claimed, assisted by a few 'maintenance' electroshocks and tranquillizers, for years.

This boy's father was known to Morel as a good man, and his son, a good boy who did not masturbate, seems to have hated him. How can the discrepancy between the public image of the father, and the experience to which the boy testifies, be resolved? Not, for Morel, by trying to

73

explore the family structure in which the boy's feelings, I would guess, would find their intelligible context. Instead, examine his head or his psyche. People have been examining the heads, blood, and urine, or the imagined *psycho*pathology of such boys and girls ever since. Some are inclined to examine heads, blood, urine; others favour pathology 'in' the 'psyche'. The hunt for the 'pathology' and the aetiology of the 'disease' goes on, as much by those concerned with psychopathology as by those concerned with physical pathology. Is it possible that his boy did not hate his father because he was ill but was turned into an invalid because his hatred for his father was invalidated?

If our wishes, feelings, desires, hopes, fears, perception, imagination, memory, dreams . . . do not correspond to the law, they are outlawed, and excommunicated. Outlawed and excommunicated, they do not cease to exist. But they do undergo secondary transformations.

If A and B are incongruent, the mind police (psychiatrists) are called in. A crime (illness) is diagnosed. An arrest is made and the patient taken into custody (hospitalization). Interviews and investigations follow. A confession may be obtained (patient admits he is ill, displays insight). He is convicted either way. The sentence is passed (therapy is recommended). He serves his time, comes out, and obeys the law in future. Some people are refractory to such methods, and their prognosis is regarded as poor. The psychiatrist, who is a specialist in these matters, can see one of those refractory cases coming.

In the last paragraph, I have given an account of the official story of psychiatric consultation, examination, diagnosis, prognosis, treatment, in terms of how it is often *experienced*. If the 'patient' refuses to accept the public definition of this situation, this shows he is under the paranoid delusion he is being persecuted by our attempt to help him to realize he is *not* being persecuted.

Most psychiatrists among the comparative few who have studied families directly, have come to the view that much psychiatric practice remains as naïve as Morel's.[1]

Who defines the situation? What is the situation? What is in fact the case, and what is not the case?

---

[1] See: Boszormenyi-Nagy and Framo (Eds.), (1965); Lidz, Fleck, and Cornelison (1965); Handel (Ed.), (1968); Cooper (1967).

Family Scenarios

The most common situation I encounter in families is when what *I* think is going on bears almost no resemblance to what anyone in the family experiences or thinks is happening, whether or not this coincides with common sense. Maybe no one knows what is happening. However, one thing is often clear to an outsider: there is concerted family *resistance* to discovering what is going on, and there are complicated stratagems to keep everyone in the dark, and in the dark they are in the dark.

We would know more of what is going on if we were not forbidden to do so, and forbidden to realize that we are forbidden to do so.

Between truth and lie are images and ideas we imagine and think are real, that paralyse our imagination and our thinking in our efforts to conserve them.

Each generation projects onto the next, elements derived from a product of at least three factors: what was (1) *projected* onto it by prior generations, (2) *induced* in it by prior generations, and (3) its response to this projection and induction.

If I project element x from set A onto element y of set B, and if we call the operation of projection or mapping ϕ, then y is the image of x under ϕ.

As we say, Johnny is the 'image' of his grandfather.

There is always a projection or a mapping of one *set* of

relations onto another *set* of relations. These are relations in time as well as space. In this type of projection or mapping, the *temporal* sequence may be retained or altered.

Projection (like other operations we shall consider later) is usually unknown to the people who are involved. Different mappings go on simultaneously.

Pure projection is not enough. As images of ghostly relations under the operation of projection, we induce others, and are ourselves induced, to *embody* them: to enact, unbeknown to ourselves, a shadow play, as images of images of images . . . of the dead, who have in their turn embodied and enacted such dramas projected upon them, and induced in them, by those before them.

One way to get someone to *do* what one wants, is to give an order. To get someone to *be* what one wants him to be, or supposes he is or is afraid he is (whether or not this is what one wants), that is, to get him to embody one's projections, is another matter. In a hypnotic (or similar) context, one does not tell him what *to be*, but tells him what he is. Such *attributions*, in context, are many times more powerful than orders (or other forms of coercion or persuasion). An instruction need not be defined as an instruction. It is my impression that we receive most of our earliest and most lasting instructions in the form of attributions. We are told such and such is the case. One is, say, told one *is* a good or a bad boy or girl, not only instructed *to be* a good or bad boy or girl. One may be subject to both, but if one *is* (this or that), it is not necessary to be told to be what one has already been 'given to understand' one is. The key medium for communication of this kind is probably not verbal language. When attributions have the function of instructions or injunctions, this function may be denied, giving rise to one type of *mystification*, akin to, or identical with, hypnotic suggestion. Hypnosis may be an experimental model of a naturally occurring phenomenon in many families. In the family situation, however, the hypnotists (the parents) are already hypnotized (by their parents) and are carrying out their instructions, by bringing their children up to bring their children up . . . in such a way, which includes not realizing that one is carrying out instructions: since one instruction is not to think that one is thus instructed. This state is easily induced under hypnosis.

One may tell someone to feel something and not to remember he has been told. Simply tell him he feels it. Better still, tell a third party, in front of him, that he feels it.

Under hypnosis, he feels it; and does not know that he has been hypnotized to feel it. How much of what we ordinarily feel, is what we have all been hypnotized to feel? How much of who we are, is what we have been hypnotized to be?

Your word is my command. A relationship of one to another may be of such power that you become what I take you to be, at my glance, at my touch, at my cough. I do not need to say anything. An attribution, as I am using the term, may be kinetic, tactile, olfactory, visual. Such an attribution is equivalent to an instruction to be obeyed 'implicitly'.

So, if I hypnotize you, I do not say, 'I order you to feel cold.' I indicate it is cold. You immediately *feel* cold. I think many children begin *in* a state like this.

We indicate to them how it is: they take up their positions in the space we define. They may then choose to become a fragment of that fragment of their possibilities we indicate they are.

What we explicitly *tell* them is, I suspect, of less account.

What we indicate they are, is, in effect, an instruction for a drama: a scenario.

For example, a naughty child is a role in a particular family drama. Such a drama is a continuous production. His parents tell him he *is* naughty, because he does not do what they tell him. What they tell him he *is*, is *induction*, far more potent than what they tell him to do. Thus through the attribution: 'You are naughty', they are effectively telling him *not to do* what they are ostensibly telling him to do. We are likely to find that such words as: 'You are naughty', are the least of it. One is likely to find that the child is being induced to behave as he is by tactile–kinetic–olfactory–visual signals: and that this is part of a 'secret' communications network, dissociated from the official verbal communiqués.

These signals do not tell him to be naughty; they define what he does *as* naughty. In this way, he learns that he *is* naughty, and *how* to be naughty in his particular family: it is a learned skill. Some children have a special aptitude for it.

I do not mean that this is the only way a child becomes 'naughty', but it is one way.

Thus:

Not: Do what I tell you *to* do
But: You will do what I indicate you *are* doing
You see what I say you see
Not: Be what I tell you to be
But: You are what I indicate you are.

The clinical hypnotist *knows* what he is doing; the family hypnotist almost never. A few parents have described this technique to me as a deliberate stratagem.

More often parents are themselves confused by a child who does *x*, when they tell him to *do y* and indicate he is *x*.

'I'm always trying to get him to make more friends, but he is so self-conscious. Isn't that right, dear?'

'He's so naughty. He never does what I tell him. Do you?'

'I keep telling him to be more careful, but he's so careless aren't you?'

When such indications or attributions[1] and instructions are discrepant, the two systems A and B are evident. If there is a smooth 'normal' state of affairs, the structure is less evident, but not essentially different. Moreover, if it all seems to work, no one is likely to want to see how it works:

'He knows right from wrong himself: I've never had to tell him not to do these things.'

'He does it without me having to ask him.'

'He knows himself when he has had enough.'

The smoothly working family system is much more difficult to study than one that is in difficulties.

*   *   *

[1] All the media of communication may carry these quasi-hypnotic indicators (attributions). The way things are said (paralinguistics) rather than the 'content' (linguistics). The movements we use (kinesics and para kinesics). And touch, taste, smell. The most intensive systematic study of kinesics has been conducted for some years by Professor Birdwhistell of Eastern Pennsylvanian Psychiatric Institute, and his associates. No systematic data, as far as I know, has been gathered on taste and smell. At the University of Florida Professor Jourard has made a beginning of a study of our touching habits (Jourard, 1968), but so far has not carried his studies into families. Dr Harry Wiener of New York Medical College has published a series of highly suggestive speculations on the way our social conduct may be partially controlled by external chemical messengers (ECM) or *ecto*-hormones, as we know the intricate social coordination of some insects to be, opening up a vast and hitherto almost entirely unexplored field of human studies: the relation of ecto-hormones to social behaviour in man (Wiener, 1966, 1967, 1968).

There are usually great resistances against the process of mapping the past onto the future coming to light, in any circumstances. If anyone in a family begins to realize he is a shadow of a puppet, he will be wise to exercise the greatest precautions as to whom he imparts this information to.

It is not 'normal' to realize such things. There are a number of psychiatric names, and a variety of treatments, for such realizations.

I consider many adults (including myself) are or have been, more or less, in a hypnotic trance, induced in early infancy: we remain in this state until – when we dead awaken, as Ibsen makes one of his characters say – we shall find that we have never lived.

Attempts to wake before our time are often punished, especially by those who love us most. Because they, bless them, are asleep. They think anyone who wakes up, or who, still asleep, realizes that what is taken to be real is a 'dream' is going crazy. Anyone in this transitional state is likely to be confused. To indicate that this confusion is a sign of illness, is a quick way to create psychosis. The person who realizes that 'this is all a nightmare' is afraid he is going crazy. A psychiatrist who professes to be a healer of souls, but who keeps people asleep, treats them for waking up, and drugs them asleep again (increasingly effectively as this field of technology sharpens its weapons), helps to drive them crazy.

The most awake people I have met are most aware of this. They are few. They are not necessarily psychotic, nor well-known intellectuals. A celebrated philosopher told me he reckons he did not awaken from this post-infancy hypnotic state till over fifty, when he had already written most of the works for which he is renowned.

Freud's *The Interpretation of Dreams* is in part an autobiographical account of his struggle to wake from that enveloping state of sleep, within which we sleep the sleep within which we dream our dreams, whose main function, in Freud's view, is to preserve sleep, but which can also be the royal road to the unconscious: that is to say, to becoming conscious.

Here is a comparatively simple example of projection or mapping. Consider the projection, not only in terms of the projec*tor* (as is usually done), but also in terms of the possible effects on the person projec*ted* upon. What may projections *induce* in the projected-upon? No one has the answer: we are answer and question.

Freud gives this account of a vision described to him by a woman of 40:[1]

One morning she opened her eyes and saw her brother in the room, though, as she knew, he was in fact in an insane asylum. Her small son was sleeping in the bed beside her. To save the child from having a *fright* and *falling into convulsions* when he saw his uncle, she pulled the sheet over his face, whereupon the apparition vanished. This vision was a modified version of a memory from the lady's childhood; and, though it was conscious, it was intimately related to all the unconscious material in her mind. Her nurse had told her that her mother (who had died very young, when my patient was only eighteen months old) had suffered from epileptic or hysterical *convulsions*, which went back to a *fright* caused by her brother (my patient's uncle) appearing to her disguised as a ghost with a sheet over his head. Thus the vision contained the same elements as the memory: the brother's

[1] Freud (1958, Vol. V, p. 545).

83

appearance, the sheet, the fright and its results. But the elements had been arranged in a different context and transferred on to other figures. [Freud's italics.]

On a superficial level, there are two sets of relations:
Set A
   her nurse
   her mother
   and her uncle, her mother's brother
Set B
   the woman herself
   her son
   and her brother, her son's uncle.

Under the operation of ϕ (see page 77) her brother appears to her in relation to her son, as (according to her nurse, according to . . . ?) her mother's brother (disguised as a ghost) had appeared to her mother.

She protects her son (ϕ mother) from her brother (ϕ uncle)

Set A	ϕ	*Set B*
mother	$\rightarrow$	son
her mother's brother	$\rightarrow$	her brother
(her uncle)		(her son's uncle)

'Her' 'mother' is the image of her nurse's image of her mother.

What ϕ value may we infer *she* may have assumed via the transformations reported?

Freud comments: 'The obvious motive of the vision, *or of the thoughts which it replaced* [my italics] was her concern lest her little boy might follow in the footsteps of his uncle, whom he greatly resembled physically.'

Freud proposes that the woman 'sees' her brother 'in' her

son, is frightened her son will take after his uncle who is mad, and overlays this projection with another, namely, of her mother as refracted to her through her nurse.

Freud sees that his patient sees her brother in her son. She is frightened her son will take after his uncle.

A little boy puts a sheet over his head to disguise himself as a ghost and scare his sister. She does not 'get over' her fright, but marries, has a son and a daughter, and dies. When her daughter grows up and has a son, she sees her brother (now in a mental hospital) appear in the room where her son sleeps; to protect her son, she puts the sheet over *his* head.

To avoid the dreadful, Freud's patient brings it about, by placing the mantle of the ghost over the head of her sleeping son.

A play with shadows. The sheet over the head of a little boy frightening his sister, is pulled over the head of his sister's daughter's son, by a niece whom he may never have met. A ghost in a story told by a nurse to a little girl of when her mother was little, haunts the life of a little boy who has yet to discover his nightmare. The sheet veils from his eyes a vision he has not yet learned to see.

Freud's patient's vision renders visible to us a tiny fragment of a veil whose texture is projection, by ourselves, from ourselves, on ourselves, of ourselves. *We* are the veil that veils us from our self.

Two intrinsic difficulties face us in studying families. First, the time scale. Families (of some kind or other, albeit *very* different from ours) have existed, say, for 100,000 years. We can study directly only a minute slice of the family chain: three generations, if we are lucky. Even studies of three generations are rare. What patterns can we hope to find, when we are restricted to three out of at least 4,000 generations?

A second difficulty is that the more smoothly they function, the more difficult they are to study.

We can take a watch to pieces and put it together again. We can invent one; learn to make one. We can find out things about it by interfering with it. And so on. Very few of the ways natural scientists have of studying the systems they study are open to us in studying families, especially those aspects of families that I am discussing with you.

We cannot expect to catch the curtain going up or down in a drama we are born into. But there are plays within plays.

Take any piece of paper. Draw anything on it. Crumple it up. Mathematically one can express precisely in what way the flat and crumpled patterns are similar and different.

The more one studies families in detail, the more it becomes apparent that patterns are spread over generations. They undergo transformations. No one, as far as I know, has found out whether *these* patterns and their transformations *can* be expressed in terms that at present we call mathematical. This is understandable. We ourselves, all of us, are ourselves the elements of the pattern we are trying to discern. Family patterns are not laid out before us like the stars in the sky.

Notes endowed with such awareness that they are only just able to glimpse the existence of the chord whose elements they are. Perhaps, from the interpretation of their vibrations they may even begin to infer something in and beyond them. We call it music; that disdains to be heard by the notes that comprise it.

We are acting parts in a play that we have never read and never seen, whose plot we don't know, whose existence we can glimpse, but whose beginning and end are beyond our present imagination and conception.

Operations

The world, as Hegel puts it, is 'a unity of the given and the constructed'. It is difficult to determine what is 'given' and what are our 'constructions'. One way is to compare the ways people in different times and places, and even in the same time and place, experience the world. All of us have been, or will be, surprised, even incredulous, when we come across the data of anthropology for the first time, at how vast are the differences between ways of experiencing.

We know very little in detail about how this comes about. We can say for certain that children are not born experiencing the world as we do, as adults, in a particular culture.

They construe the original 'given' in ways we as adults once have done, but have forgotten. The study of early childhood experience is very difficult: children cannot tell us, in our language, how they experience, and we often cannot remember.

Our adult experience is a very sophisticated product of many procedures.

The laws governing our experience, I presume, are both natural and social. At a certain level of realization, we distinguish between natural and social laws.

'The Mesopotamian Universe – because it did not consist of dead matter, because every stone, every tree, every conceivable thing in it was a being with a will and character of its own – was . . . founded on authority; its members, too, willingly and automatically obeyed orders which made them act as they should act. These orders we call the laws of nature.'[1]

The 'deeper' social laws are implanted; the more 'hard-programmed' or 'pickled' into us, the more like 'natural' laws they come to appear to us to be. Indeed, if someone breaks such a 'deeply' implanted social law, we are inclined to say that he is 'unnatural'.

The following are a few allusions to some seemingly 'natural' features of contemporary experience, acquired when we are very young.

We construe the given in terms of *distinctions*, according to *rules*. We perform *operations* on our experience, in order to comply with the rules. By these operations, according to the rules, in terms of the distinctions, a product is generated.

We make distinctions, but are not born with the distinctions we make ready made.

I suppose there to be a set of primitive distinctions in terms of which we construe what presents itself: and our first differentiated experiences to be the first product of our most primitive constructions and the *virgin* given. This product subsequently *appears* to be given. Compared to our adult experience, this 'original' experience is 'virginal' or innocent. *Any* experience wherein the given is distinguished in any way, is not innocent and not given, though it may seem to be. We are free to apply our terms in different ways, but our set of terms is as determined for us as the phonemes (sound units) of our language.

[1] Professor Thorkild Jacobsen: quoted in Hooke (1962, p. 78).

I suppose such distinctions to be acquired, and acquired early.

A set of primitive distinctions are formed.

Rules govern the formation of this set and the operations performed on this set.

I guess that by one year from birth the following distinctions, among others, have come to be made:

1. inside and outside
2. pleasure and pain, pleasant–unpleasant
3. real and not-real
4. good and bad
5. me and not-me
6. here and there
7. then and now.

For present purposes it is immaterial at what age these distinctions have been made: or even what the distinctions are. *Some* distinctions come to be *made*, somehow or other, some time or other: these distinctions did not exist in the first place. With these distinctions, we work upon the *prima materia* of the given. Our experience is a product, formed according to a recipe, a set of rules for what distinctions to make, when, where, on what. Rules are themselves distinctions in action. Operations between distinctions already constructed are carried out continually according to further rules.

I slice my experience into inside–outside: real–unreal: good and bad: me and not-me: here and there: now and then; I find it pleasant or painful.

Let us suppose: inside–me–here–now–good–real–pleasant applies to the same slice. You may feel I am lucky. This does not mean that if all me is good, all is real is me: nor that if

I am here–now, I was not there–then. But I do have an 'identity' very highly prized in our culture. Me–unreal–bad–here–inside–now–pain is not unusual.

One of our fundamental distinctions is inside and outside. It cannot be considered for long in isolation from the other distinctions we make: this distinction (as all others) operates with other distinctions according to rules for their combination. The inside–and–outside distinction is applied to almost all facets of experience. I can hardly *not* make this distinction. Very seldom will I drop it. Imagine the following actions:

  (i) swallow the saliva in your mouth
 (ii) take a glass of water: sip it and swallow it
(iii) spit in it, swallow spit and water
(iv) sip some water: spit it back, sip, and swallow what you have spat back.

You may be able to do all four, easily, but many people cannot, and are disgusted especially at (iii) and (iv).

One is aware that there is a difference between saliva inside one's mouth, and that same saliva, one inch in space outside one's mouth.

There is an even sharper differential in terms of faeces, inside or outside.

We feel ourselves to be inside a bag of skin: what is outside this bag is not-us. Me – inside. Not-me – outside.

In ecstatic moments, this distinction is lost. Making love, starvation, listening to music, high fever. Few have not experienced its loss, but few have experienced its loss often, or for long (such is my impression).

These moments are privileged exceptions. Under usual circumstances inside–outside is one of the distinctions which, combined together with other distinctions by rules of an experiential syntax, seem to help towards giving us a sense that our experience makes sense. It belongs to the familial–social order, not to the natural order.

Yet the syntax of common sense is as obscure as it is obvious. In a modern city, we may prefer to take for granted that I am inside my skin and outside yours, and you are inside your skin and outside mine!

But difficulties arise. 'I' am inside my skin, but I may feel outside what is inside me and outside all I am not inside. Where then am I? Not quite inside anything? Not quite outside anything? What do I want to be inside? What do I want to be outside? What do I want to be inside me? What do I want to be outside me? Do I want to be inside what is inside me? Do I want to be outside what is inside me? Do I feel inside what is outside me? Is what is inside me, what I would like outside me? Is what is outside me, what I would like inside me? Perhaps I can do an exchange. By projection, put what is inside me, outside me. By introjection, put what is outside, inside. I have now turned myself inside-out and outside-in. But, despite this exchange I may still feel outside the inside, and inside the outside. Let us introduce the good–bad distinction. Suppose my insides were bad, and by projection I have put them outside. My bad insides, now outside, persecute me. Or suppose I want to get outside what *I* am inside. Difficult, without finding that I have what *I* was inside, inside me. A doubtful improvement. If I am full of goodies inside, they may be stolen by those who have no goodies like me. If I put the goodies outside, then I am empty of goodies, and am dependent for my supplies of goodies from the outside. The attempt to find a satisfactory stable combination between good–bad, empty–full, inside–outside, me–not-me, may take up a great deal of energy – so

I shall feel exhausted, empty inside *and* outside. Suppose we add, real and unreal, true and false, to this infernal dance: to be real is to be genuine, and to be unreal is to be false. I must avoid being unreal, but if I am *inside* reality, reality may be outside, and if I am already empty inside, I may find myself in danger of being empty, unreal, false, and bad. But I *want* to be full of reality, true and good. Let's do another exchange. Immediately it is Them who are false, empty, unreal, and bad.

But it is not everyone who finds a resting-place this way. Suppose to be real is to be *inside* the real, but the outside is unreal because I have put the real inside. So try to put the outside inside again, make the inside real, make the real full, and the full genuine. Then I am good because I am full but bad because I am not full of myself, hence unreal. But can we not distribute things a bit more evenly?

Surely there is enough reality to go round? Let us say: inside me is real, and inside *them* is real. It is real outside me and I am inside reality, and reality is inside myself. So where is unreality? Unreality does not exist, and does not *deserve* to exist.

We, our family and our family's families, our school, our church, our town, our state and our country, our television and cups and saucers and display cabinet, and our Aunt Jessie, are real: and true; we can trust each other: and we have a full life. The world comes to our town; and if we sometimes do wrong: we do our best. We don't wish any evil on anyone. We *are*. And those to whom *we* do not exist, do not exist, and if we can help it, shall not exist.

Because we must defend *reality* against the emptiness, deceit, and the evil, of *Unreality*. That is what we are fighting for. To defend the real against the unreal, the true against falsehood, the full life against an empty life, the good against evil. What is, against what is not.

But then, what are we defending ourselves against? Nothing? Oh no! The danger, the menace, the enemy, Them, are very real. So we have to start again. . .

They Are Real. They are dangerous, because they *are*. So long as they *are*, we are in danger. So we must destroy them. If we must destroy them, they must destroy us to prevent us destroying them, and we must destroy them before they destroy us before we destroy them before they destroy us . . . which is where we are at the moment.

They may seem unreal and nonexistent, real and exist, unreal and exist, or real and not exist. *They* exist to be destroyed and are destroyed to be reinvented.

We need not worry that the kill ratio between Them and Us will get too high. There are always more where *they* came from. From *inside Us*.

Given our distinctions and our rules, we have to *work* to normalize our experience. We could never succeed unless we were able to employ a further set of operations on our experience to some of which I have already alluded. Most of these are described in psychoanalysis as 'defence mechanisms'.

Denial is one of the simplest.
    'This is the case' is changed to: 'This is *not* the case';
    e.g. 'I feel jealous' is changed to: 'I do *not* feel jealous.'
Splitting. A set is partitioned into two subsets.
    In a complete split, no traffic is allowed to occur between the two subsets.
Displacement
    e.g. I feel angry at Tom, *instead* of Dick. I come back

and 'take it out' on the wife, for what I feel about the boss.

Scotomatization

I do not see what I do not want to.

Replacement

I see something else instead.

Projection

I map inside onto outside.

Introjection

I map outside onto inside.

Rationalization

I give myself a cover-story.

Repression

Forgetting and forgetting one has forgotten.

Regression

Going back

Identification

Two separate subsets are taken to be one.

Mystification

Misdefinition of the issues.

Reversal

I hate him is reversed to: he hates me.

Many more are described in psychoanalytic literature, including inversion, reaction-formation, isolation, reduplication, turning against the self, undoing, idealization, derealization.

The definitive work remains to be written on this subject. The present list is not well classified, because some of these 'defences' are simple, and others made up of two or more simple operations. The subject is a very difficult one in the technical literature; there are overlaps in connotation between terms: different authors do not use the same term in the same way: the literature is in three principal languages: German, English, and French, giving rise to problems of translation. Freud's own theorizing, in this and other respects, evolved and changed through over forty years.

Operations apply additional constraints on the product. They 'cancel' and substitute what is in accord with rules, and they do this according to rules that govern the operations themselves. If experience (E) is permitted to be pleasant or *ought* to be pleasant, E will be operated upon to make it more seemingly pleasant. But if the rules do not permit or demand this, if pleasure is forbidden or despised, then 'pleasure' will be sacrificed for other values higher in the hierarchy.

Most operations on E are themselves operated upon to render them as we say 'unconscious'. Only as we manage to neutralize these operations on operations can our operations on E become themselves elements of E, such that we can examine them. Until we can do this, we have to *infer* them. Such an inference as to their existence may itself be blocked by such operations as denial, scotomatization.

The operations on experience under discussion are commonly not experienced themselves. So seldom does one ever catch oneself in the act that I would have been tempted to regard them as, themselves, *essentially* not elements of experience, had I not occasionally been able to catch a glimpse of them *in action* myself, and had not others reported the same to me. It is comparatively easy to catch someone else in the act. This leads me to propose that there is an operation, or a class of operations, that *operates on our experience of our operations*, to cancel them from our experience: operations of this latter class somehow operate on our experience of *themselves*, in such a way that we experience neither our first operations nor the operations that shut the former operations out of our experience. This is particularly clear in the case of repression.

When I was thirteen, I had a very embarrassing experience. I shall not embarrass you by recounting it. About two minutes after it happened, I caught myself in the process of putting it out of my mind. I had already more than half forgotten it. To be more precise, I was in the process of sealing off the whole operation by forgetting that I had forgotten it. How many times I had done this before I cannot say. It may have been many times because I cannot remember many embarrassing experiences before that one, and I have no memory of such an *act* of forgetting I was forgetting before thirteen. I am sure this was not the first time I had done that trick, and not the last, but most of these occasions, so I believe, are still so effectively repressed that I have still forgotten that I have forgotten them.

This is repression. It is not a simple operation. We forget something. And forget that we have forgotten it. As far as we are subsequently concerned, there is nothing we have forgotten.

A clean-cut operation of repression achieves a *cut-off*, so that

(a) we forget X
(b) we are unaware that there is an X that we have forgotten
(c) we are unaware that we have *forgotten* X
(d) and unaware that we are unaware that we have forgotten we have forgotten X.

Repression is the annihilation, not only *from* the memory of, but *of* the memory of, a part of E, *together with*, the annihilation of the experience of the operation. It is a product of at least three operations.

When we consider any actual instance of any operations, we find that it is almost impossible to find a pure example of a single operation in isolation. This is what we might expect. It does not mean, because a baby moves all the fingers of one hand at once, that it has not five fingers. Denial and displacement form a common operation product. 'It's not *my* fault. It's your fault.' Denial and displacement can equal projection.

Wish-fulfilment and idealization are varieties of operation entailing projection and denial. All projection involves some measure of denial of the range of E. I am unhappy. I am *not* unhappy (denial). I am *not* denying that I am unhappy (denial of denial).

I take the principal function of all these operations to be: the production and maintenance of E that is at best desired, at least tolerated, in the family by the family in the first place.

The operations I have alluded to are operations on one's own experience. They are done by one person to himself or herself. But they would be unnecessary unless the rules of the family required them: and ineffectual unless others co-operated. Denial is demanded by the others: it is part of a *transpersonal system of collusion*, whereby we comply with the others, and they comply with us. For instance, one requires collusion to play 'Happy Families'. Individually, I am unhappy. I deny I am to *myself*; I deny I am denying anything to *myself* and to the others. They must do the same. I must collude with their denial and collusion, and they must collude with mine.

So we are a happy family and we have no
secrets from one another.
If we are unhappy/we have to keep it a secret/
and we are unhappy that we have to keep it a secret
and unhappy *that* we have to keep secret/the fact/that we
have to keep it a secret
and that we *are* keeping all that secret.
But since we are a happy family you can see
this difficulty does not arise.[1]

Repression of much infant sexuality is sanctioned, the act of repression is itself denied, and repression, its sanction, and the denial of repression, are denied. Nothing has happened. 'I don't know what you're talking about.' For instance, who ever heard of a good boy, and a normal man, *ever*, having wanted to suck his father's penis? It is quite normal, at one time, to have wanted to suck his mother's breast. However, it is on the whole best not to connect mother's breast and girl friend's breast, or, if one is a woman, woman's breast with boy friend's genitals. It is safest, on the whole, to keep these sets of relations in separate partitions (splitting), and *repress*, to be even more on the safe side, *all infantile desires* in case they were too 'perverse', since they antedate partitioning and repression, etc., *and* to deny the existence of any such operations of partitioning and repression, and to deny this denial. The product arrived at is the outcome of many rules without which it could not be generated or maintained, but to admit the rules would be to admit what the rules and operations are attempting to render nonexistent.

One is expected to be capable of passion, once married, but not to have experienced too much passion (let alone

[1] For a few more of this sort of thing, see Laing (1970).

acted upon it) too much before. If this is too difficult, one has to pretend first not to feel the passion one really feels, then, to pretend to passion one does *not* really feel, and to pretend that certain passionate upsurges of resentment, hatred, envy, are unreal, or don't happen, or are something else. This requires false realizations, false de-realizations, and a cover-story (rationalization). After this almost complete holocaust of one's experience on the altar of conformity, one is liable to feel somewhat empty, but one can try to fill one's emptiness up with money, consumer goods, position, respect, admirations, envy of one's fellows for their business, professional, social success. These together with a repertoire of distractions, permitted or compulsory, serve to distract one from one's own distraction: and if one finds oneself overworked, under too great a strain, there are perfectly approved additional lines of defence, concoctions to taste of, narcotics, stimulants, sedatives, tranquillizers to depress one further so that one does not know how depressed one is and to help one to over-eat and over-sleep. And there are lines of defence beyond *that*, to electroshocks, to the (almost) final solution of simply removing sections of the offending body, especially the central nervous system. This last solution is necessary, however, only if the *normal social* lobotomy does not work, and chemical lobotomy has also failed.

I can think of no way of generating a 'normal' product from the stuff of our original selves except in some such way: once we arrive at our matrix of distinctions, we have rules for combining and partitioning them into sets and subsets. The 'normal' product requires that these operations themselves are denied. We like the food served up elegantly before us: we do not want to know about the animal factories, the slaughterhouses, and what goes on in the kitchen.

Our own cities are our own animal factories; families, schools, churches are the slaughterhouses of our children; colleges and other places are the kitchens. As adults in marriages and business, we eat the product.

Rules and Metarules

Generally, we are very aware of our distinctions but not nearly so aware that we *make* them. Operations on E are usually not experienced. Yet with their help most of us flesh out a world of sorts. With great labour, a wish is

  (i) denied
 (ii) replaced by a fear that generates a nightmare that is
(iii) denied, and on which a
(iv) façade is then placed
(denial, replacement, denial, replacement) – a comparatively simple, four-step sequence.

Such operations may be *demanded*. Projection and the denial of it is demanded. It is mandatory to project bad onto what is the Enemy whoever they may be: and it is *mandatory* to deny that this is projection.

One can lay out a *projection* map for the whole cosmos, shaded or coloured as to what regions we must or must not project what onto: a map for a map.

To take the simplest schema. Let us suppose each region is governed by a rule about good–bad. Suppose values for each region are set as (+) good, or (−) bad, (+ or −) optional, or neutral (0, neither + nor −).

There is said to be a *time* and place for everything. At home:

  1. one must *not* put mother's pearl necklace down the w.c.

2. one *must* put something down the w.c. and nowhere else
3. one must *not* go to bed with one's boots on
4. one *must* brush one's teeth before going to sleep
5. one must *not* make bad smells at the dinner table and

so on. Such rules are liable to be exact and stringent.

Rules governing values to endow the cosmos may also be stringent.

There are times and places and people for

1. + values (good)
2. − values (bad)
3. + or − values (optional)
4. neither + nor − (o) values (neutral)
    (the stars must be regarded as neither good nor bad).

We can add an open fifth category for regions one may regard as good (+), or bad (−), or optional (+ or −), or neutral (o). They are few.

If there is perfect coincidence between the values projected on and allotted to a range, everything is in its proper time and place. There is no infringement of the rules on this set of issues, and no need for guilt or anxiety on these grounds.

When positive values are mapped on a positive range, one thinks well of those one is supposed to think well of. If one is a Christian, God is Good. If one is a Patriot: One's Country is Good. If one is a Black Powerite: the Blacks are Great. One is good oneself if one has good thoughts about what one is supposed to think good about, and bad thoughts about what one is supposed to think bad about. When negative values are mapped onto the positive range, one does not think well of those one is supposed to think well of. When negative values are applied to the negative range, one thinks badly of those one is supposed to think badly about. With positive values to the negative range, one thinks well of those one is supposed to think badly of. With positive or negative values to the optional range, one thinks badly or well of what or of those one is free to take sides over. Neutral values to the neutral range, one does not think well or badly about what one is supposed to think is neither good nor bad. And so on.

Such rules govern the whole social field. Unless we can 'see through' the rules, we only see through them. They make social science a peculiarly difficult subject, because the social scientist in one particular society does not simply dissolve the rules because he is a social scientist. 'We' can easily see that there is little place for sociology in Russia or China. It is much more difficult for us to see how 'our' rules govern the values we map onto the social field. It is difficult even to see that we have values we are mapping, let alone see the rules in terms of which such projections are carried out.

In terms of such rules for what values we endow what regions of the world, that is, in terms of our projection map, let us consider evil thoughts.

Evil thoughts are a relationship. It is not what you think, see, feel, intend, imagine, etc., but *what* you think, etc., *about what* or *whom*, when and where.

It is bad to think bad about what you are supposed to think good about. It is bad to think good about what you are supposed to think bad about. It is good to think *bad* about what you're supposed to think *bad* about. It is a bit mad to take seriously what is not supposed to be serious. It is bad to be frivolous about what one is supposed to be serious about (inappropriate affect). A 'good' or a 'bad' thought, only becomes Good or Bad in relation to its object: *what* we are thinking about *what*. A bad thought is *good* if applied to a bad object. A good thought is *bad* if applied to a bad object.

Without any knowledge whatever of the target person or range, we in our society *know* what attributions we should/ should not apply to whom: father, mother, husband, wife, son, daughter, self; Whites, Reds, Yellows, Blacks, Jews, Goyim; good–bad, safe–dangerous, trustworthy–untrust-worthy, kind–cruel, and so on.

Once any part of the social world system comes to be governed by such rules, each part of the social world system

(i) is endowed with a value by the fact that there is a rule governing it.

(ii) There may be a rule that this value must not be changed, challenged, *questioned*, or even *seen*.

(iii) There may be a rule not only against *seeing* that there *is* such a value, and that there is a rule (i), but

(iv) there may be a rule against seeing (ii) and

(v) a rule against seeing (iii) and

(vi) a rule against seeing (iv) and (v) and (vi).

There are rules against seeing the rules, and hence against seeing all the issues that arise from complying with, or breaking, them.

Breach of rules, and rules against seeing rules, and rules against seeing rules against seeing rules, is met by deterrents in the first place, to forestall any breach of the system, and punishments in the second place.

But neither deterrence nor punishment can be defined as such in *words*, since such a definition would itself be a breach of the rules against seeing the rules . . .

The direct breach of basic rules at the first level can be punished by death. The person earns attributions of treason, treachery, heresy: he is liable to be seen as being evil, wicked, depraved, degenerate. People commonly feel that no punishment is good enough for him: he or she ought to be horsewhipped: *and* given the very best treatment: he or she is *bad* and mad (Ezra Pound for example).

Writing about talking about rules about rules about rules, as I am doing, is possible, if not pushed too far, or too direct. To push further, to be safe, I must become more *abstract*.

Rules govern all aspects of experience, *what* we are to *experience*, and what *not* to experience, the operations we must and must not carry out, in order to arrive at a permitted picture of ourselves and others in the world.

Suppose we are told to repair a car engine: given instructions that inevitably lead to the engine falling apart: and we are instructed to feel *bad* if it is *not* put together.

One may be instructed, if things seem to be going wrong, to examine one's instructions. They may be wrong. They may require adaptation, modification, or to be dropped. But a special situation exists if there is a rule against examining, or questioning rules: and beyond that, if there are rules against even being aware that such rules exist, including this last rule.

If *what* we are instructed to achieve cannot be achieved by the *how* we are instructed to achieve it, we are in difficulties.

We are instructed to be honest. But instructed to operate on our experience in ways that can only be called dishonest.

We are instructed to be trust*ing* of certain others, who tell us that we cannot trust ourselves. So that we are called on to place our untrustworthy trust in those who tell us to trust them when they tell us that we are untrustworthy: hence, our trust is untrustworthy. And so on.

People carry out different operations according to different sets of instructions, to maintain much the same primary distinctions (in our culture) mapped onto the social cosmos, strictly according to the rules. According to what these distinctions are applied to, and how they are applied, different worlds of experience are generated and maintained. If the instructions are contradictory or paradoxical they may lead to distinctions being combined in simultaneous and incompatible sets.

It can happen that it is not even possible to *split* or partition the world into two, three, or more bits so that each subset consists of compatible elements.

There are instructions as to *what* we experience. And instructions as to *how* we have to experience what. As with our behaviour. We are told, for instance, to brush our teeth (what to do). And we are told *how* to do so.

Instructions give us more or less responsibility and more or less discretion. For instance: we may be instructed to keep our teeth and gums in good repair. It may be left to our discretion how we do so. If our teeth get rotten, it may or may not be our fault, according to whether we have been instructed to regard this as our responsibility. However, if we are instructed to clean our teeth in a specific way, with a specific sort of toothbrush and a specific type of toothpaste, to eat certain things that are good for the teeth and not to eat other things that are bad for the teeth, together with other specific dos and don'ts, and if we do the dos and don't do the don'ts – if, that is, we carry out our instructions to the letter – then, *if* our teeth fall out, it is not our fault. But we must search ourselves to find where we have gone wrong, if not in the letter, then in the spirit of the way we carried out our instructions. If things go wrong, so we may have been instructed, it is a punishment. It behoves us to find the crime that fits it. And if we do not find the crime, this failure is a crime. It only serves to show how criminal we are. Our teeth may be falling out, therefore, because although we have eaten precisely what we should have and no more than we should, we have *wanted* to eat more or otherwise. Maybe it is a punishment for our greed. Clearly we would be unwise to be wise only *after* the event. So we shall have to go over our instructions 'with a fine tooth comb' all the time, in search of any fault that might be punished by our teeth falling out, or worse. But is this constant self-examination not itself a fault: a form of self-indulgence, or narcissism, egotism, pride, self-importance? What else can one do, created frail, commanded to be sound? We must pray. But would we not be wise to have all our teeth removed, both to avoid them falling out, and to mortify our flesh for its self-indulgence and our spirit for its sins against the flesh? For especially if one cannot find what they are, one has been instructed to realize that such failure betokens the greatest depth of sin: to be so sunk in depravity that one cannot even see one's depravity. If one cannot see one's depravity, this failure to see one's depravity is a depravity more depraved than all other depravities. . . .

No one intended, when they told a little boy when and how to clean his teeth, and that his teeth would fall out if he was bad, together with Presbyterian Sunday School and all the rest of it, to produce forty-five years later the picture of a typical obsessive involutional depression. This syndrome is one of the specialities of Scotland.

Two or more instructions may be incompatible. This

engenders, at least viewed structurally, a comparatively simple type of conflict. I tell you to do both A and B, but you can't do the one if you do the other. We can become tied in much more complex knots. I can do no more than indicate some aspects of this subject, which is only beginning to be studied by a few people.[1]

If I tell you to do something, this does not explicitly tell you to tell yourself that you are doing it because I told you. I may tell you to do something and be prepared to let you tell yourself (if you wish, if it makes you feel any better) that you are doing it because you want to, *not* because you have been told to. On the other hand, *you* may want to do something, but see that I like to feel that you want to do what I tell you, so you get me to tell you to do what you want to do, so that you will be doing what you want, and what you are told at the same time.

However, this may embarrass me, so I order you to (i) do what *I* want (ii) but among the things I want is that you, in doing what *I* want, do not *think* that you are doing what I want, but that you are doing what *you* want, and, even, far from that being what I want, it is what I *don't* want. So I instruct you, in carrying out my instructions which are not what you want but which are what I want, to tell yourself that: on the contrary, you are doing what you want and not what I want.

On top of all this, orders may not only be contradictory, incompatible, or disguised, they may be paradoxical. A paradoxical order is one which, if correctly executed, is disobeyed: if disobeyed, it is obeyed. Don't do what I tell you. Don't believe me. Be spontaneous.

[1] See especially Watzlawick, Beavin, and Jackson (1967).

I have been able to observe real-life family situations that embody all the above possibilities, and others.

The situation is complex, but once one begins to break some of the rules against seeing the rules, one realizes that much of one's difficulty is not due to the intrinsic complexity of the subject but to one's inhibitions against seeing what may be obvious, once the inhibition against seeing it is undone. There remain inhibitions against putting into words such real or imagined insights.

I have never come across anyone (including myself) who does not draw a line as to: *what may be put into words*, and, *what words what may be put into*.

If my view is right, we at this moment may not know we have *rules against knowing about certain rules*.

Some of you sense that you have rules about rules, but perhaps have never thought about it in these terms.

Some of you are clear this far. You will have to bear with me, for a little, before I get to where you are at, if I can.

I want to talk about the rules that we cannot talk about – just enough to convince any of you who are not sure what I am talking about that this is a very important issue, which I cannot talk about more directly.

There is a law against murder. We can talk about murder, and about the law about murder.

There is a law against incest. We can talk about the law against incest, rather more freely than we can talk about incest: commonly there is a rule against talking about incest, in front of the children especially: but not an absolute rule against talking about whether or not there is a law against incest.

It used to be obvious to many (including Lévy-Bruhl)

that when incest does not happen it is because there is a 'natural' revulsion against it. To many, it may now seem equally obvious that it does not occur more frequently because there are rules against it.

Many people used to be scandalized by this view, for it seems to imply that, if there were not such rules, people might do what was prohibited. Many people felt, and some no doubt still do, that to admit that there were rules against incest would be to admit that parents and children, and brothers and sister, might *want* to have sexual relations with each other. Why should there be a rule against what no one 'naturally' wants to do? Freud's view was that what people think they 'naturally' don't want to do *may* be a product of repression, and other operations, at the behest of rules against even thinking much less doing it. The desire, even the thought, *and* the rule against the desire or thought, are all eliminated from our awareness, so that the product of these operations on oneself is a 'normal' state of awareness, whereby one is unaware of the desire, the thought *and* the rules, and the operations.

One tends to assume that every negative rule (such as that against incest) implies a prior desire, impulse, propensity, instinct, tendency to do it. Don't do that, implies that one would be inclined to if not forbidden.

There is treasure at the bottom of the tree. You will find it. Only remember not to think of a white monkey. The moment you do, the treasure will be lost to you forever. (A favourite story of Francis Huxley.)

We can, by direct experiment, verify that some negative injunctions have a paradoxical effect, to induce one to do what one has been told not to, *especially if one did not*, and does not, in fact, wish to.

'I would never have thought of it until I was told that I must not.'

Negative rules may themselves generate actions they prohibit. If you want people not to do something they are not doing, do not forbid it. There is a better chance that I will not think what I have not yet thought, if you do not tell me *not* to.

In this last minute, I have not been trying to establish whether or not incest is ruled out by social rules or natural law, or both. I have wished only to demonstrate that there is not a rule against talking *about* whether or not there are such rules or such a natural law.

A family has a rule that little Johnny should not think filthy thoughts. Little Johnny is a good boy: he does not have to be told not to think filthy thoughts. They never have *taught* him *not* to think filthy thoughts. He never has.

So, according to the family, and even little Johnny, there is no rule against filthy thoughts, because there is no need to have a rule against what never happens. Moreover, we do not talk in the family about a rule against filthy thoughts, because since there are no filthy thoughts, and no rule against them, there is no need to talk about this dreary, abstract, irrelevant, or even vaguely filthy subject. There is no rule against talking about a nonexistent rule about nonexistent filthy thoughts: and no rule against talking about nonexistent talk about a nonexistent rule about something that is nonexistent.

Perhaps no one outside such a family rule system could knowingly embrace it—

Rule A: Don't. Rule A1: Rule A does not exist. Rule A2: Rule A1 does not exist.

This type of ruling applies only to some rules. One can

talk about certain rules (when one can cross the street). But there are others that one cannot talk about without breaking the rule that one should not talk about them.

If you obey these rules, you will not know that they exist. There is no rule against talking about putting one's finger into one's own mouth, one's brother's, sister's, mother's, father's, anyone's mouth. No rule against *talking* about putting one's finger into the custard pie, though there *is* a rule about putting one's finger into the custard pie. No rule against recognizing the rule: don't put your finger into the fire. Why not? Because you will burn yourself. There is no rule against *talking* about it and giving reasons for it.

But, I may say, I have never put my finger into a number of . . . (unmentionable) places.[1] What places? I can't mention them. Why not? When one cannot talk about a rule about which one cannot talk, we have reached a limit to what we can talk about.

I have thought about the problem of how not to think a thought one is not supposed to think. I cannot think of any way to do so except, in some peculiar way, to 'think' what one must not think in order to ensure that one does not think it.

'Of course', it never would even occur to a perfectly brainwashed person to think certain unmentionably filthy thoughts. Such cleanliness, however, requires constant vigilance: vigilance against what? The answer is strictly unthinkable. To have clean memories, reveries, desires, dreams, imagination, one must keep clean company, and

[1] 'Unmentionable' only in relation to what cannot be related to it (my finger) in this particular context.

guard all senses against pollution. If one only overhears someone else talking filthy, one has been polluted. Even if one can forget one ever heard it, right away. But one has to remember to continue to forget and remember to remember to avoid that person in future.

Many such rules about rules apply to what parts of whose body can be 'thought' of in relation to whom.

Rules apply to what kinds of sensations one is supposed to have where and when in one's own body, in relation to whom.

What are the funny places where funny feelings go on? Where do they come from? Where do they go to?

One seeks to avoid painful feelings, but there are many pleasurable feelings many people are forbidden to experience, imagine, remember, dream about, and they are definitely forbidden to talk about the fact that they are forbidden to talk about them. This is easy if one has already obeyed the injunction not even to 'think' of what I can possibly be talking about.

One has then got to the position in which one cannot think *that* one cannot think about what one cannot think about because there is a rule against thinking about X, and a rule against thinking that there is a rule against thinking that one must *not* think about *not* thinking about certain things.

If some thoughts cannot be thought: and among the thoughts that cannot be thought is the thought that there are certain thoughts that cannot be thought, including the aforementioned thought, then: he who had complied with this calculus of antithoughts will not be aware he is not aware that he is obeying a rule not to think that he is obeying a rule not to think about X. So he is not aware of X and not aware that he is not aware of the rule against being not aware of X. By obeying a rule not to realize he is obeying a rule, he will deny that there is any rule he is obeying.

When one does no more than scratch the surface of the structure of one of the varieties of Western 'conscience', one must marvel at its ingenuity. It must constitute one of the biggest knots in which man has ever tied himself. One of its many peculiar features is that the more tied in the knot, the less aware are we that we are tied in it.

Anyone fully caught in the full anticalculus of this kind cannot possibly avoid being bad in order to be good. In order to comply with the rules, rules have to be broken. Even if one could wash out one's brain three times a day, part of one's self must be aware of what one is not supposed to know in order to assure the continuance of those paradoxical states of multiplex ignorance, spun in the paradoxical spiral that the more we comply with the law, the more we break the law: the more righteous we become the deeper in sin: our *righteousness* is as filthy rags.

Mapping

The inverse operation to projection is introjection.

Both are mapping operations, whereby elements and relations between elements from one set, called the domain, are mapped onto elements and relations between elements called a range.

There can be many different mappings from one set into another. There can be mappings of one set into itself.

To recall: if ϕ is a mapping of A into B, set A is called the domain of ϕ, and set B the range of ϕ.

Projection is a mapping of inside onto (or into) outside, and introjection a mapping of outside onto inside. Families are of peculiar significance because, more than any other social set, they are both domain and range, for projections *to* outside, introjections *from* outside, *and*, they are the range for *projections* to them *from* the members of the family itself, as they are the domain of introjections to individuals in the family. Projections onto the family, from family members, combined with introjections onto them from outside, are combined to form a product which is in turn further projected and introjected: such projections and introjections are in turn introjected and projected, endlessly.

One's body is of unique significance because it is *the* range for 'introjective' mappings from all domains: and these introjective sets provide a 'pool' for projections in turn *to* any domain, from which re-introjections and re-reprojections and re-re-reprojections and re-re-re-introjections, can be, and *are*, carried on without end. However, in practice the contingency possibilities are restricted considerably, as we know, of *what* may be mapped onto *what*. This we shall have to examine.

The family supplies the principal *domain* from which introjective ϕ maps are made. The *nexification* of the family is the intensive mapping again and again of $F \rightarrow F \rightarrow F \rightarrow F \ldots$ within the sets and subsets of the network of whole persons and part-object familial relations, over generations.

The family is also the *range* for introjective mappings *from* domains outside the family. These family introjections are the domain from which the baby and infant is subject to fantasization. The infant is the *final common range*, as it were – where all introjections converge and permutate, are pooled and stored to become a sort of ϕ *bank*, the subsequent *domain*, *from* which subsequent projections will be released (according to some curious chronometer whose nature we have yet to determine), to find *their range*, anywhere from a marital relation, a nuclear family, a social network, to the *total social world system*, or even the total cosmos.

The social world system as range, with its subsets already multiply mapped by projections, becomes in turn the domain from which, through the family, introjective mappings are concentrated, once more to be reprojected . . .

One should in no way be deterred by difference of magnitude between domain and range. One can project a minute domain onto a vast range; or a vast domain onto a minute range. *Scale* is no deterrent in practice (cf. astrology, palmistry, alchemical medicine; man, the microcosm, as 'image' of macrocosm: possible analogy with holograms, and so on.) It is not a question of the 'scientific' truth, or value, of such mappings. We are however in the true realm of science when we study what these mappings are. They exist no less today than before. But they are very inadequately studied 'scientifically', whether by psychologists or sociologists, or anthropologists, when it comes to 'ourselves' rather than 'primitive' societies.[1]

The operation whereby this mapping is done, is usually 'unconscious'. People describe what is an image of an image of an image, but they do not realize that this is what it is, taking it instead to be some sort of primary reality.

In order to develop this theory further, we would need to make an incursion into the mathematical theory of mapping, and this must be deferred for another time.

Suppose I projected my mother onto my wife. She takes on the ϕ-value of my mother *for me*. That is projection. However (cf. the Clarks, above) I may or may not *induce* her to embody my mother. The operation of inducing her to embody my projection is what I am calling *induction*. Projection is done by one person as his *own* experience of the other. *Induction* is done by one person to *the other's* experience. We have actually no word for the transformation of the *other's* experience under such induction. Introjection is an operation *by* me on *my* experience, which is identical in principle with projection, the only difference being that the locations of the transference are different, namely: from any region of what is taken to be not-me, or not-self, or not that with which I identify myself (e.g. my family), *onto* what I take to be 'me', 'self', or that with which I identify myself.

It is not sufficient to say that my wife introjects my mother, if by projection, and induction, I have manoeuvred

[1] See Willis (1967).

her into such a position that she actually begins to act, and even to feel, like her. She may begin to act and feel like her without ever having met her. Indeed, it is quite possible for my actions to induce another to feel and act like someone I myself may never have known.

Let us take a fictitious example in which I shall use the first person only for simplicity. My father lost his mother when he was a boy and was brought up by his older sister. His wife was rather a big sister – cum–mother – to him. He never had a daughter, and I knew he missed one. When I get married he finds in my wife the mother he lost, and this fits her own image of herself derived from her mother and father. By this convergence of projections upon her, she is finally induced to be more than a mere image for such projections: she becomes the very embodiment of someone (or an amalgam of persons) she has never met, or even hardly heard of. She having been induced to become my father's mother, whom does that tend to induce me into? My son into? My daughter into? And so on.

Such inductions are going on, in my view, all the time. All our actions and reactions to the other imply some coefficient of induction. We very seldom ever entirely relate absolutely accurately to the other. And indeed very seldom is there another there to whom one could. We make a gesture, that is itself an induced embodiment of an image of another *of* another projected upon oneself by another; this gesture in turn induces more or less compellingly from the other to whom we address it a complementary gesture; this last gesture induced by my induced gesture, induces in *me* in turn a gesture that responds by a further induction . . . and so the play goes on.

*　*　*

I have tried to reveal a state that becomes more so the less it is recognized.

This is a difficult state to live through. We are prepared to be happy or unhappy, satisfied or frustrated, hopeful or despairing, good or evil. As long as we know where we are: as long as we feel orientated. We think we know *where*, what, when, who, even how and why we are.

We would rather be anywhere, as long as we are somewhere. We would rather be anyone, as long as we are someone.

We can *cling* to being a Christian, a married man, a housewife, a dutiful daughter, to attributions, even unpleasant ones. One is not that to which one seems to be clinging.

Our family of origin has done its best. It has given us its range of distinctions, options, identities, definitions, rules, repertoires of operations, instructions, attributions, loci, scenarios, roles, parts to play . . .

But it has not told us who are 'we' who play those parts and take up those positions.

Some of you may feel that I have recklessly generalized from particular instances of 'pathology' to the 'normal'. Since I have met hardly any of you who may hear or read this, I must leave you to take or leave what you may find in what I've said that may seem interesting or relevant to you. Here is one last example, which I offer to suggest that the gap between what seems to be abnormal or deviant or pathological, and what does not, may be more superficial than it appears at first encounter. This is a conversation between a mother and her fourteen-year-old daughter.

M (to fourteen-year-old daughter): You are evil.

D: No, I'm not.

M: Yes, you are.

D: Uncle Jack doesn't think so.

M: He doesn't love you as I do. Only a mother really knows the truth about her daughter, and only one who loves you as I do will ever tell you the truth about yourself no matter what it is. If you don't believe me, just look at yourself in the mirror[1] carefully and you will see that I'm telling the truth.

The daughter did, and saw that her mother was right after all, and realized how wrong she had been not to be grateful for having a mother who so loved her that she would tell her the truth about herself. Whatever it might be.

This example may appear somewhat disturbing, even sinister. Suppose we changed one word in it: replace 'evil' by 'pretty'.

M: You are pretty.

D: No I'm not.

M: Yes, you are.

D: Uncle Jack doesn't think so.

M: He doesn't love you as I do. Only a mother really knows the truth about her daughter, and only one who loves you as I do will ever tell you the truth about yourself no matter what it is. If you don't believe me, just look at yourself in the mirror carefully, and you will see that I'm telling you the truth.

The *technique* is the same. Whether the attribution is pretty. good, beautiful, ugly, or evil, the *structure* is identical. The structure is *so* common that we hardly notice it unless the

[1] Compare Winnicott (1967) and Lacan (1966).

attribution jars. We all employ some recognizably similar version of this technique and may be prepared to justify it. I suggest that we reflect upon the *structure* of the *induction* not only the *content* thereof.

What, I think, we find most immediately disturbing about this can be expressed in general terms as follows: the other person induces self to map into self's own image of self a value which, we feel, should not be mapped onto self; the self-system is a range that should not, we may feel, be mapped in that way, in any circumstances or only under extreme circumstances.

Nevertheless, if it was another value we felt to be more 'appropriate', we might not feel disturbed. Further: if a child were taught to map the same value, 'evil', onto a region regarded as the *proper* range for such a value, that also would not, I think, disturb us.

Hitler was an evil man, for example. We teach our children this, and many similar things, before they can possibly make up their own minds from 'the evidence'. We may feel that someone is positively evil if he does *not* feel that Hitler was an evil man. Take racism: semitism; anti-semitism; anti-anti-semitism. Blacks and Whites. Black Anti-Whites. White Anti-Blacks. White trash and Niggers. 'Anyone who thinks in that way is worse than they are.' Black Anti-Anti-Whites. White Anti-Anti-Blacks. Even those of us who think we do not employ such values tend still to use them, but they are now reserved for those who employ them.

'I don't think the Whites are any more degenerate, essentially, than us Blacks. But anyone who talks about Niggers is really White trash.'

'I don't think the Whites are superior to the Blacks,

essentially, but those Blacks who incite violence and talk about "White monkeys", are no better than monkeys themselves.'

As long as we cannot up-level our 'thinking' beyond Us and Them, the goodies and baddies, it will go on and on. The only possible end will be when all the goodies have killed all the baddies, and all the baddies all the goodies, which does not seem so difficult or unlikely since, to Us, we are the goodies and They are the baddies, while to Them, we are the baddies and they are the goodies.

Millions of people have died this century and millions more are going to, including, we have every reason to expect, many of Us and our children, throttled by this knot we seem unable to untie.

It seems a comparatively simple knot, but it is tied *very, very* tight – round the throat, as it were, of the whole human species.

But don't believe me because I say so, look in the mirror and see for yourself.

Bibliography

BIBLIOGRAPHY

BATESON, G. (1961) *Perceval's Narrative: A Patient's Account of his Psychosis*. Stanford University Press, Stanford, Calif.

BOSZORMENYI-NAGY, I. and FRAMO, J.L. (Eds.), (1965) *Intensive Family Therapy*. Harper and Row, New York.

COOPER, D. (1967) *Psychiatry and Anti-Psychiatry*, Tavistock Publications, London.

ESTERSON, A. (1970) *The Leaves of Spring*. Tavistock Publications, London.

FOUCAULT, M. (1965) *Madness and Civilization. A History of Insanity in the Age of Reason*. Pantheon Books, New York; Tavistock Publications, London.

FREUD, S. (1958) *Standard Edition*, Vol. V. Hogarth Press, London.

GOFFMAN, E. (1961) *Asylums: Essays on the Social Situation of Mental Patients and Other Inmates*. Doubleday-Anchor Books, New York; Penguin Books, Harmondsworth.

HALEY, J. (1965) 'The Art of being Schizophrenic.' *Voices*, I.

HANDEL, G. (Ed.) (1968) *The Psycho-Social Interior of the Family: A Source Book for the Study of Whole Families*. Allen and Unwin, London.

HOOKE, S. H. (1962) *Babylonian and Assyrian Religion*, Blackwell, Oxford.

JOURARD, S. M. (1968) *Disclosing Man to Himself*. Van Nostrand, New York.

LACAN, J. (1966) 'Le stade du miroir comme formateur de la fonction du Je.' In *Ecrits*, Editions du Seuil, Paris.

Translation: 'The Mirror-phase as formative of the Function of the I.' *New Left Review*, No. 51, 1968, pp. 71–77.

LAING, R. D. (1965) 'Mystification, Confusion and Conflict.' In: Boszormenyi-Nagy and Framo (Eds), op. cit.

LAING, R. D. (1967a) *The Politics of Experience*. Penguin Books, Harmondsworth; Pantheon Books, New York.

LAING, R. D. (1967b) 'Individual and Family Structure.' In P. Lomas (Ed.): *The Predicament of the Family*. Hogarth Press London.

LAING, R. D. (1969) *Self and Others*. Tavistock Publications, London; Pantheon Books, New York.

LAING, R. D. (1970) *Knots*. Tavistock Publications, London; Pantheon Books, New York.

LAING, R. D. and ESTERSON, A. (1964) *Sanity, Madness, and the Family: Families of Schizophrenics*. Tavistock Publications, London; Basic Books, New York. Second edition 1970.

LAING, R. D., PHILLIPSON, H., and LEE, A. R. (1966) *Interpersonal Perception. A Theory and a Method of Research*. Tavistock Publications, London; Springer Publishing Co., New York.

LIDZ, T., FLECK, S., and CORNELISON, A. R. (1965) *Schizophrenia and the Family*. International Universities Press, New York.

MOREL, B. A. (1860) *Traité des maladies mentales*. Librairie Victor Masson, Paris.

SCHEFF, T. (1967) *Being Mentally Ill*. Aldine Books, Chicago.

SPECK, R. V. (1966) 'Psychotherapy of the Social Network of a Schizophrenic Family.' *Family Process*, Vol. VI, No. 2.

SZASZ, T. (1961) *The Myth of Mental Illness*. Harper, New York.

WATZLAWICK, P., BEAVIN, J. H., and JACKSON, D. D.

(1967) *Pragmatics of Human Communication. A Study of Interactional Patterns, Pathologies and Paradoxes.* Norton, New York.

WIENER, H. (1966, 67, 68) 'External Chemical Messengers' Parts I to V. *New York State Journal of Medicine*, Vols. 66, 67, 68.

WILLIAMS, C. (1950) *The Descent of the Dove.* Faber & Faber, London.

WILLIS, R. G. (1967) 'The Head and the Loins: Lévi-Strauss and beyond.' *Man*, No 4, pp. 518–534.

WINNICOTT, D. W. (1967) 'Mirror-role of Mother and Family in Child Development.' In P. Lomas (Ed.): *The Predicament of the Family.* Hogarth Press, London.

ZARLOCK, S. P. (1966) 'Social Expectations, Language and Schizophrenia.' *J. human Psychol.*, Vol. 6, No.1, p. 68.

Index

INDEX

R. D. Laing studied medicine at Glasgow University. He was a psychiatrist in the British army and a physician at the Glasgow Royal Mental Hospital, and taught at the University of Glasgow. Subsequently, he joined the Tavistock Clinic and was later appointed Director of the Langham Clinic in London. From 1961 to 1967 he undertook research into families and he is now in private practice as a psychoanalyst.

As a psychoanalyst and psychiatrist, his research has been concerned with extreme disturbances in human communication, with different kinds of families, and with the varieties of human experience.

He is the author of numerous articles and reviews. His other books include *Self and Others; The Divided Self; Reason and Violence* (with David Cooper); *Sanity, Madness and the Family* (with Aaron Esterson); *Interpersonal Perception: A Theory and a Method of Research* (with H. Phillipson and A. R. Lee); *The Politics of Experience;* and *Knots.*

VINTAGE WORKS OF SCIENCE AND PSYCHOLOGY

VINTAGE POLITICAL SCIENCE AND SOCIAL CRITICISM

VINTAGE BELLES—LETTRES